You
Don't Know
My
Story!

Testimonials and Words
of Encouragement

Candice Rasco

ISBN 978-1-63844-155-7 (paperback)
ISBN 978-1-63844-156-4 (digital)

Christian Faith Publishing, Inc.
832 Park Avenue
Meadville, PA 16335
www.christianfaithpublishing.com

Scriptures and quotes are from https://www.biblegateway.com,

Serenity Prayer: https://www.beliefnet.com/prayers/protestant/addiction/serenity-prayer.aspx#ybv2W06FXWrWb-Va4.99

https://www.google.com/search?client=opera&hs=pyD&q=-Dictionary#dobs=mirage

Printed in the United States of America

To Edith Chavous Rasco, my grandmother, who took the time out to teach me how to lean on and trust God. She was the biggest influence in my life.

CONTENTS

INTRODUCTION

My name is Candice Rasco Veal, and I was born in Chicago, Illinois, to Grover Reed and Linda Rasco in September 5, 1978. I was raised in Hillsboro, Mississippi, and now reside in Illinois. As a child, I became no stranger to hardship, hurt, pain, and abuse. As a young adult and as an adult, I learned the hard way that big hearts get broken, and being too nice without a balance can lead you into dangerous situations.

As an adult, I dealt with sexual assault, abuse, homelessness, having a child taken from me, and domestic violence. I've had people I love and trust turn their backs on me when I needed them the most. Through all that, had it not been for God being there for me even when I didn't know, He was there—I didn't die or lose my mind.

I started to journal a long time ago as a teen and kept it up, and I decided to write this book to share some of my life experiences, my testimonies, and how I made it through in hopes that someone will read this and know that you too can make it. I am not a scholar, and I don't have a master's or a doctrine degree.

I am just a simple wife and mother who has been through hell and back, who knows that there is a God and that God has saved my life so many times. In this book, I am making my life an open book to you so you can see that God truly cares. And just as He has and is working it all out for me, He can do the same for you.

Chapter 1

STARTING OUT

I have come to learn that God can save whoever He desires to when he desires and how He desires. He is not confined to this box that we sometimes try to place Him in. He is way bigger than that. As a child of the Most High God, we have to understand a few things: One is that we have to know that the only way to God is through Jesus.

Yes, Jesus is the redeemer of the saints. And if you claim to be a believer—a child of God—then you must come to the realization that you cannot accomplish that without first acknowledging that Jesus is Lord and the Messiah, the true sacrificial Lamb of God. When you have acknowledged that Jesus is Lord, and you have accepted Him truly and completely into your heart and your mind, then it is time to accept Him into your soul.

The Word says in Romans 10:9: "If you declare with your mouth, 'Jesus is Lord,' and believe in your heart that God raised him from the dead, you will be saved." When you accept Him (Jesus), you go on in obedience and then get baptized in the name of the Father, the Son, and the

Holy Spirit—some say Holy Ghost (I say Spirit because God Himself is a Spirit, being so I feel more comfortable with saying Holy Spirit).

After all this is done, they say, "Oh well, begin to study to show thyself approved so that you will know for sure who you are and whose you are." The Bible says in Matthew 6:33 (KJV): "But seek ye first the kingdom of God and his righteousness; and all these things shall be added unto you." God is a loving Father and would never leave His children ignorant. So the seeking is solely for our benefit.

We need to learn all there is to know about our destiny as a born-again child of God. As a baptized child of God, we know that we are reborn renewed. The old us died, and we rose up out the water a new creation. As a new creation, we are joint heirs with Jesus, and we can claim victory in our lives just as He did because of His sacrifice for us on the cross. You may ask well: How can one be victorious in all that they do? Well allow me to tell you.

We are victorious through our obedience. True victory comes through obedience. This is very import that we understand this. We have to have faith in the God that we serve, and then we have to choose to follow His will and His way in true obedience. Obedience to God unlocks the full manifestation of the blessings He has for us.

A lot of people don't fully seem to understand this, or they try to go around it, but you can't. We have to be obedient to God's will and His ways. It's hard to be obedient to God if you are not willing to humble yourself and submit and if you don't love God.

Every believer always says, "Oh, I do love God. I love Jesus. But the Word says in John 14:15(KJV): "If you love me, keep my commandments". This is how we show that we love God by submitting to the word and will of God in obedience. He shows His love for us daily through His mercy and His grace.

We need to understand that God doesn't see love as just mere words. He searches the heart of each believer and pays attention to the things that we do, because love is an action word. Jesus showed us His love for us through His sacrifice. That was an action. And we have to show our love through our actions with each other daily.

It is also beneficial to us to know that the God that we serve is a God of order. He has a way of doing things in a structure. He doesn't deviate, and God doesn't change. He is the same today, yesterday, and forevermore. We must have faith that the Lord, out of His magnificence, will accomplish what He said that He would in our lives.

We are all here for a particular purpose that God knows alone. And in order to understand what it is that He needs us to do, we must seek His face daily and have faith and believe in Him at all times—yes, in all times, the good the bad and the ugly times that we go through in this life. We have to have faith and just keep on trusting God to lead the way. Yes, trusting in God can seem difficult in the bad times. But if we meditate on the goodness of God, He will give us perfect peace.

He will give us a peace that surpasses all understanding. I am a living witness to this very thing. I was going through one of the hardest times in my life. I was homeless with two kids going to college. Trying to work and be a mom was very challenging to me. I truly thought that I was going to lose my mind.

I remember crying out to God, "Please help me." But I stayed reading the Word and seeking God. And even though I was sleeping in cars on park benches and riding the "L" in Illinois all night because I had nowhere to go, I chose to trust

God. I had no other choice. I knew from whom my help came from. So I did lift up my eyes to heaven and sought out God for deliverance, and He gave me peace and let me know that weeping may endure for a night, but yes, joy comes in the morning.

I just had to keep pressing for that dawn to break forth in my life, and it did. I have endured many hardships including assault and abuse, but God was a constant positive influence in my life, keeping me through it all. Jesus was a friend to me when everyone else turned their backs on me. When family deceived me and let me down, I had Jesus.

He would always show up right on time. That's how I know we serve an on-time God, because when I thought all hope was gone, God would show up and show out for me. Will it be easy? No, nothing in this life is easy. Somewhere along the way, we all will experience struggle some more than others, and this can either be for two reasons: You are disobedient, or it is part of God's will and purpose for our lives.

I know, through experience with God and the Holy Trinity, that when I chose to be obedient, I would see a change in my life. But when I was operating in my flesh, my life was twirling in a downward spiral fast, and I was being hit at every area in my life. I was so tired of going through in this life that one time I allowed the enemy to speak to me and convince me to take my own life, but God intervened in such a way I knew it had to be God.

This is how I know that when the enemy comes in like a flood, the Lord, our God, will come in our lives to lift a standard that we do not drown. The Word of God says in Isaiah 59:19(AKJV): "So shall they fear the name of the Lord from the west, and his glory from the rising of the sun. When the enemy shall come in like a flood, the Spirit of the Lord shall lift up a standard against him." In 1 Corinthians 10:13, the

Word says, "No temptation has overtaken you except what is common to mankind. And God is faithful; he will not let you be tempted beyond what you can bear. But when you are tempted, he will also provide a way out so that you can endure it."

God wants us to be victorious. He won't let us fail as long as we allow Him to lead the way and not continue to always want to do the things we feel we want to do. You may wonder, *Well how can I receive this help, this power, this anointing that I need so much in my life?* Well I'm glad that you asked, because I have the answer. In order to receive the things that God had for us, we have to position ourselves to receive it.

We have to align our lives up with the word and the will of God. And when we do that, we will see the change we need to see in our lives. Remember, God is a God of order. And when we follow His order and design for our lives, He blesses us. When we don't do what the Word of God says, we miss out on the important things that God needs for us to get and understand His will for our lives individually, as well as collectively.

God has a plan for you, for me, for everyone. And in order to know what that plan is, we have to consult with the Alpha and the Omega, the Creator of all creation. That alone is amazing that someone that powerful knows us and wants to have an intimate, personal relationship with us. He wants to be involved in our everyday lives. I find that to be so fascinating, and it makes me want to be closer to a love that strong.

God looks only for us to be obedient to Him. Out of all the things that He does for us, all He wants is our hearts and respect and loyalty. These are very simple things considering all that God does for us on a regular basis that we don't even realize that He is doing, all the doors that He has opened and sealed shut for our benefit, the secrets that he has kept and will never reveal to another soul, the blessings He stays giving out, the mercy, and the grace that He has issued out so freely. He is always busy helping and keeping us all. And all He desires is for us to love Him and be obedient to His will and His way which, if we look at it, benefits us the most anyway.

He just wants to see us prosper, like any loving parent wants for their child and/or children. We are exactly that—His children, His creation. And when we gave our lives to Him, we were supposed to have begun a new life, following Jesus to be more like Him and less like the world we came out of. We are children of the Most High God and are supposed to be set apart.

Question is: If we are calling ourselves disciples or Christians, can the people in the world tell the difference? If not, then that's where the problem lies. My grandmother used to always say, "You can't straddle the fence in this life. You have to go to either side. I have heard also that saying: You can't go to heaven holding the devil's hand. You have to pick a side.

The Bible says in Revelation 3:16 (KJV): "So then because thou art lukewarm and neither cold nor hot, I will spue thee out of my mouth." I would do the same. Just think about it. If you were to order ice water in a restaurant, and they just bring you a glass of tap water—no ice—you will send it back. Or if you order hot coffee or hot food, and they bring it to you warm—you will send it back. You want what you asked for, nothing in between. But what you asked for, well that's what God is saying: He wants us to be for Him and only Him.

Chapter 2

FREE INDEED

The Bible says in the Christian Standard Bible (CSB) from Joshua 25:15: "But if it doesn't please you to worship the *Lord*, choose for yourselves today: Which will you worship—the gods your fathers worshipped beyond the Euphrates River or the gods of the Amorites in whose land you are living? As for me and my family, we will worship the *Lord*."

God created us with free will so that we could choose to do right from wrong and good instead of evil and so that we can see Him for Who and What He is to us in our lives and freely give ourselves to Him and worship Him in Spirit and in truth. I remember going through losing my daughter because I was fighting homelessness, and her father's mother took her and told me that when I got on my feet, I could come get her back. Well that was a lie.

Her and her daughter ended up going behind my back and forging a letter and took my daughter to court and told them I left her on the steps and never came back for her. I was there every day, and they never said a word to me until I tried to leave with my daughter. Then she told me she had guardianship of my daughter. I felt like someone took a sledgehammer and hit me dead in the chest. I walked away feeling lost and betrayed and angry. I cried and cried and cried. I cried out to God asking for help.

I asked Him how He could allow this to happen to me. I was getting bitter as time passed. I felt like given up. My baby was gone, and I didn't know how I was going to get her back. Well after a while, God showed me where it all went wrong and how my decisions led to those He clearly told me not to do. That was the first time I learned that it's best to be obedient. Because when we obey our flesh, we get ourselves into situations that sometimes takes a while to get out of.

When I left that day, my daughter was five. It took me nine years in and out of court to get her back. I had to actually ended up cutting her own father loose because the judge told me that he was the reason I couldn't get my daughter back. He was a toxic person, and so was his family, and God needed me to get myself together and free my life of all of them. And when I did, everything just started to fall in place rapidly. And just like that, she was with me where she belonged. I went through what seemed like the gates of hell just to get my baby back. But it was well worth it.

Looking back over that journey in my life, I saw from the start to the finish of it all, how God was there for me even when I thought He wasn't. I saw how every time I got myself caught up and bound, He would lose the shackles that had me bound. And He would keep reminding me, "Candice, you are free." I was being attacked from every end, and I would hear, "You're free, whom the Son set free is free indeed. You are free, my child. Come up out of this." I learned that I made things harder for myself than it had to be.

All I had to do was listen and be obedient. It also reminded me of the situation in the Bible when the Israelites took forty years because they decided to grumble and complain. It is so easy to rebel against the Lord and to do things the way that we want to. But there will come a time when we will have to choose what we do and have to be ready and willing to live with that choice no matter the outcome.

With that in mind, I implore us all to just take the time to make better decisions pertaining to our lives and our souls. We can always trust God even though we can't trust ourselves or even those who we hold near and dear to our hearts. Why? You may ask. It's because God is a God that will never fail us. He is Jehovah-jireh, our provider.

God, through Jesus our Lord and Savior, made a commitment to forgive us and to give us the opportunity to have a new life and a new beginning through Jesus's sacrifice made on Calvary. Just as God was committed and Jesus was committed, we too have to be committed to serve the Lord our God with all that we have in us.

He wants it all—our hearts, minds, bodies, our soul, and our resources. Our father is the Creator of the universe and isn't weak. So since we are His children, then we have to realize that He has equipped us, and therefore we are not weak either. God doesn't just tell us what it is that He can do, He shows us.

He shows us through His actions, thus, the reason why in His word He says, "Faith without works is dead" (James 2:26 NIV). As the body without the spirit is dead, so faith without deeds is dead. We have to not be just hearers of the word of God, but we must also be doers of the word of God.

But don't just listen to God's word. You must do what it says. Otherwise you are only fooling yourselves. For if you listen to the word and don't obey, it is like glancing at your face in a mirror. You see yourself, walk away, and forget what you look like. But if you look carefully into the perfect law that sets you free, and if you do what it says and don't forget what you heard, then God will bless you for doing it. (James 1:22–25 NLT)

We have to be dedicated and determined, as children of God, to walk out His perfect will for our lives collectively, as well as individually. We have Jesus as the perfect example to go by. He was focused on fulfilling His purpose, and He didn't allow anything or anyone to detour Him from doing what He knew was needed.

Did he want to do it at times? No. Because if you look at the situation at the Mount of Olives, He was in turmoil about what He had to go through so much that he sweated blood through His pores.

Jesus Prays on the Mount of Olives

Jesus went out as usual to the Mount of Olives, and the disciples followed Him. When He came to the place, He told them, "Pray that you will not enter into temptation." And He withdrew about a stone's throw beyond them where He knelt down and prayed, "Father, if You are willing, take this cup from Me. Yet not My will, but Yours be done." Then an angel from heaven appeared to Him and strengthened Him. And in His anguish, He prayed more earnestly, and His sweat became like drops of blood falling to the ground.

When Jesus rose from prayer and returned to the disciples, He found them asleep, exhausted from sorrow. "Why are you sleeping?" He asked. "Get up and pray so that you will not enter into temptation. (Matthew 26:36–46, Mark 14:32–42)

He had second thoughts just as we do, but He pressed His way through and decided that His obedience to God outweighed His feelings at the time. And just as the angels came to strengthen Jesus, if we seek God, He will dispatch angels to us, and the Holy Spirit will strengthen us to do whatever it is that God has said that we are to do.

It was through this great sacrifice that Jesus made for us that we are free indeed. No matter what we are feeling or are being told, when we elected to give our lives over to God, we become a new creature a free person. Don't forfeit your freedom. It was paid at a great price of sacrifice.

Chapter 3

What's on the Inside Will Show on the Outside

How many times have you ever heard your elders say, "Tighten up and get it together child, because what's on the inside of you will come out." They were saying that if you have a good heart and practice doing the right things, it will show. And if you aren't pure in heart and do those things you ought not to do, it too will show.

You can't hide your true nature for long. Sooner or later, it will come out. I have come to learn that this is so true in so many ways, but we will just look into what the Word has to say about it.

> Jesus said to them, "If God were your
> Father, you would love me, for I have

come here from God. I have not come
on my own, God sent me. Why is my
language not clear to you? Because you
are unable to hear what I say. You belong
to your father, the devil, and you want to
carry out your father's desires. He was a
murderer from the beginning, not holding to the truth, for there is no truth in
him. When he lies, he speaks his native
language, for he is a liar and the father of
lies." (John 8:42–44 NIV)

What we practice will show up in us. Who we follow
will also show up in us. If we then, as children of the Most
High God, would just seek God daily and meditate and pray
and apply the word of God to our lives, people will begin to
see more of the light of our Father shining through clearly
instead of just glimpses of Him here and there in our lives.

I don't know how many times I have said to myself and
others that we, as mankind, truly make things harder than
what they have to be in this life. We are going to go through
in this life true enough just as Jesus went through, and those
before us went through the storms of life as well. Just because
things don't happen for us the way that we want them to
doesn't mean that it's time to give up along our journey.

I am not just saying something that I myself haven't had
come to the realization of for myself. I was that person that
tried my best to do right and live right, and then *bam*, I was
hit with the right hooks of life, left and right. There were so
many times that I was so tired of going through that I said,
"Forget it, I quit." I would try to do my own thing. But the
thing about that is I learned you cannot unknow what you

know, and it made me feel uncomfortable trying to engage in the things I used to before I became saved.

I then started to feel sorrow for myself, and the Holy Spirit let me linger there for just a bit and then spoke to me saying, "Okay, Candice, now get up from here and press forward. You have work yet to do."

I would get up every time, shake it off, hold my head up high, and jump right back in, picking up where I left off in my journal, each time more determine to get it right the next time. It doesn't matter how many times you fall along your journey. What matters is that you don't stay down. God knew we wouldn't be perfect. That's why we have His mercy and grace that's fresh and new to us every day, and we also have the covering of the blood that Jesus shed and Him interceding for us to God.

The enemy will get in your head and make it seem like all hope is gone when sometimes that is furthest from the truth. Whenever God opens our eyes each day, there's hope. There is a reason for all things. And people will try to convince you in this life either way. But you have to understand that God expects for us to utilize the tools He has provided for us in this life to shed much light to the world.

He wants us to know that quitting is not an option when dealing with Him. I was seventeen years old, and I was so over going through—yes—at that young age. I was bitter and hurt from going through abuse as a child, and I felt I had no one to love and/or appreciate me. I felt like I didn't matter. So the enemy crept into my mind and whispered, "You know, no one loves or cares about you, so you might as well just kill yourself. No one is going to miss you if you die." I was so weak and tired at the time. Sadly, I listened.

I went into my sister's bathroom, and I took a bottle of prescription meds. I then went into my nephew's room and started to talk to him as I loved him, and I wanted my time to be spent with the person I loved. He saw something wasn't right and went to go get help.

While he was gone, I heard, "Go stick your finger down your throat and vomit those pills up."

I said, "No, I want to die."

It said it again and again. I said no. I heard the voice a third time. This time it was sterner, and it said, "Go stick your fingers down your throat and throw those pills up now. You are pregnant with your son."

When I heard that, I ran to the bathroom and threw up the pills and went to the hospital where they indeed confirmed what I heard. I was eleven weeks pregnant and later found out it was indeed a boy!

The Bible says that the enemy comes to kill, steal, and destroy. And just like that, the enemy would have taken two souls had I not listened and obeyed the voice of God. I would have committed murder and suicide. And at that time, I hadn't given my life to Christ yet. It pays to listen to that small, still voice. God has been with me all of my life, aiding me and helping through the good the bad and the ugly in my life. The enemy has also been there trying to get me to give up and in along the way.

From that point in my life, I wanted to know more about that voice. So while pregnant and ashamed, I went to church when I was about seven months with my son. And that day was the turning point of my life. It began my walk with God.

He is twenty-two years old, and I have been walking with God for twenty-two years now. It was not an easy twenty-two years. There were traps set along the way, but the Word of God and my prayer life and my intimate relationship with the Holy Trinity have seen me through the years, still sane when other would have lost their minds, alive when others would have died.

Everything that we need, as children of the Most High God, is right there on the inside of us. And all we have to do is tap into that power. We cannot afford to allow the attacks and schemes and plots of the enemy prevail in our lives. We have to feed or souls the right things. We have to feed or mind the right food and surround ourselves with the right people.

When you listen to the ushering of the Holy Spirit, and you utilize the Word of God in your life, you'll begin to see things change for the better. As you see this change, you then have to begin to change your surroundings and the people you deal with or you allow in your inner circle. The Word of God says in 1 Corinthians 15:33 (NIV): "Be not deceived: evil communications corrupt good manners."

Basically, whatever you give yourself to whatever you yield your energy to, it will manifest in a positive or a negative way, all depending on what you do. What's on the inside of you will show up and come out. Question now is, Now that you know this, what are you going to do about it?

Are you going to continue to allow your life to remain the same, or are you going to take control of your life and make a conscious decision to live a life that resembles and shows that you are a child of the Most High God? To whom do you belong? Do you belong to God, or do you resemble Satan?

Chapter 4

IF YOU ONLY TRUST HIM

T rust—this is a word that so many of us have an issue with. Rather, it is with trusting ourselves or others or even trusting in God the truth of the matter that most of us have some serious trust issues. The reason for many of the trust issues is that we have come from the fact that we put all our hope and/or faith in someone or something and we were failed. God is asking, "Who told you that you are broken?"

How did we allow someone else who has faults and flaws to make us feel less than what God has said that we are and that we can be? How many times have you heard someone say, "Stop setting yourself up to fail." I was told this throughout my life only because I cared more about what people thought than how God thought about me and what I thought about myself.

I was hurt so many times in my life. I truly felt like I was never going to be anything else in life but a footstool for people. I began to become hardened and untrusting of everyone and everything, including God. It's normal to lose hope and faith in people because they let us down, but God never wanted us to ever lose faith and hope and trust in Him and who He is to us in our lives.

These scriptures touch on how God feels about us trusting people and trusting Him.

> It is better to trust in the *Lord* than to put confidence in man. (Psalms 118:8 KJV)

> Trust ye not in a friend, put ye not confidence in a guide: keep the doors of thy mouth from her that lieth in thy bosom. (Micah 7:5 KJV)

> Thus saith the *Lord*; Cursed (be) the man that trusteth in man and maketh flesh his arm and whose heart departeth from the *Lord*. (Jeremiah 17:5 KJV)

> It is better to trust in the *Lord* than to put confidence in princes. Psalms 118:9 KJV)

> For if a man thinks himself to be something when he is nothing, he deceiveth himself. (Galatians 6:3 KJV)

> And he hath put a new song in my mouth, even praise unto our God: many shall see it and fear and shall trust in the *Lord*. (Psalms 40:3–4 KJV)

Woe to them that go down to Egypt for help and stay on horses and trust in chariots, because they are many; and in horsemen, because they are very strong; but they look not unto the Holy One of Israel, neither seek the *Lord!* (Isaiah 31:1 KJV)

Trust in the *Lord* with all thine heart; and lean not unto thine own understanding. (Proverbs 3:5–6 KJV)

Abide in me, and I in you. As the branch cannot bear fruit of itself, except it abide in the vine; no more can ye, except ye abide in me. (John 15:4 KJV)

God never intended on any of us to lean on and trust each other to the point that when we are let down by each other, it seems too much to go on in life. God wants us to have faith and believe that if we put all our trust in Him, and Him alone, that He will never fail us, leave us, or forsake us.

I had a person tell me, "Well how can I just put my total faith and trust in someone I can't see? I live in a world with real things going on in my life. And I need real answers." I understood and said, "Well I learned everything I know through life experience. And when I was at my lowest points in life, because I trusted people who betrayed me, I tried God. And when I did, my life began to change."

I started trusted God to lead me. And when I did, He place the right people in my life to help me get to where I needed to be. He placed the right people in my life to bless me, but it wasn't until I actually looked to Him for help.

Everything that we do is a choice we choose to do or not to do a thing. We can simply choose to trust God or continue to do what we have been doing and keep getting disappointed by people.

It's okay to have a little leery feeling. He knows it's hard for people to trust in what they don't see, but that's where faith steps in. "Now faith is the substance of things hoped for, the evidence of things not seen" (Hebrews 11:1 KJV).

Do you remember the story of ole doubting Thomas? John 20:24–29 (KJV) tells this story.

> But, Thomas, one of the twelve called Didymus, was not with them when Jesus came. The other disciples therefore said unto him, We have seen the Lord. But he said unto them, Except I shall see in his hands the print of the nails and put my finger into the print of the nails and thrust my hand into his side, I will not believe. And after eight days again, his disciples were within and Thomas with them: then came Jesus, the doors being shut, and stood in the midst, and said, Peace be unto you. Then saith He to Thomas, Reach hither thy finger and behold my hands; and reach hither thy hand and thrust it into my side: and be not faithless but believing. And Thomas answered and said unto him, My Lord and my God. Jesus saith unto him, Thomas, because thou hast seen me, thou hast believed: blessed are they that have not seen and yet have believed.

Thomas was a dedicated disciple of Jesus, and yet his faith wavered. He knew Jesus up close and personal. But still when it came down to him trusting his own eyes, he couldn't; he needed proof. And Jesus was a bit disappointed in that and said in John 20:29 (KJV): "Jesus saith unto him, Thomas, because thou hast seen me, thou hast believed: blessed are they that have not seen and yet have believed."

We are the Children of the Most High God. And with that being said, we accepted Jesus as our Lord and personal Savior, so we are supposed to know Jesus is exactly who He says He is. And that no matter what we are going through or what we see or can't see, we are to know that we can trust God to do what only He can in each of our lives. He told us we can trust Him, and He told us we can look to Him for all things.

> I will lift up mine eyes unto the hills from whence cometh my help. My help cometh from the Lord, which made heaven and earth. He will not suffer thy foot to be moved: he that keepeth thee will not slumber. Behold, he that keepeth Israel shall neither slumber nor sleep. The Lord is thy keeper: The Lord is thy shade upon thy right hand. The sun shall not smite thee by day, nor the moon by night. The Lord shall preserve thee from all evil: he shall preserve thy soul. The Lord shall preserve thy going out and thy coming in from this time forth and even forevermore. (Psalms 121:1–8 KJV)

The Word of God is informative. Anything and every-thing that we need to know is right there. That's why He tells us to study the Word to seek His face and to trust Him. All that we need is in Him. He knows all and sees all. He sits high and looks low, and He is the Alpha and the Omega. And we can be assured that no matter what, in God we can trust.

Chapter 5

COUNT IT ALL JOY

All my life, I used to hear my elders tell those who were going through to count it all joy, and I never thought much of it. I thought that it was just an old saying that old people say when things don't go as planned in life. Little did I know, that phrase was going to be words I learned to live by. Let us take a look at what the Word of God has to say about having joy in our lives.

Trials and Temptations

> Consider it pure joy, my brothers and sisters, whenever you face trials of many kinds, because you know that the testing of your faith produces perseverance. Let perseverance finish its work so that you may be mature and complete, not lacking anything. If any of you lacks wisdom, you should ask God who gives generously to all without finding fault, and it

will be given to you. But when you ask, you must believe and not doubt, because the one who doubts is like a wave of the sea, blown and tossed by the wind. That person should not expect to receive anything from the Lord. Such a person is double-minded and unstable in all they do. (James 1:2–8 NIV)

These verses say so much. Why must we count it all joy regardless of the things that we go through? Well each thing we go through is a teachable moment if we allow it to be.

We are supposed to learn from the test and the trials we face in this life. As a babe in Christ, I didn't fully understand this. I thought that God was punishing me for the wrong that I had done. I wasn't looking at the fact that God was trying to strengthen me and build character in me.

I didn't understand that God was preparing me for my future. I looked at it as God was mad at me, but God was actually concerned about me and was equipping me to walk into my purpose. If you don't go through anything, how then will you know how good God is? *He* was not trying to watch me fail, He was trying to set me up to stay winning and to be victorious in all I do in life.

He was trying to give me wisdom, knowledge, and understand, because in this life, there are people and situations that would come into my life that would provoke and lead me to do things that would either build me up or tear me down. As a child of God, as a disciple of Jesus, I needed to let God and His word be the basics on how I lived my life and not allow people of the world to influence me but rather be the type of person that influence people.

I needed to trust God with all my heart, my mind, and my soul. I needed faith to do what God wanted me to do. I had to learn to wait on the Lord and His perfect timing. I went through so that I could see others through. That is the purpose of our testimonies. The things I went through made me seek God and His word or help. I spent time in the Word of God looking for answers, looking for hope, looking for inspiration and encouragement.

I learned that the love of God never changes, that no matter what I was faced with, He loved me and that I needed to show that same love to those He placed in my life along my path. He wanted me to elevate. God passes us on to the next level when we have learned to let go and to press forward, not allowing the enemy to win. I needed wisdom on how to let things and people go.

Some people are just not meant to go forward with us. Some people are just there in our lives to hold seasonal positions. And when it's their time to go, we have to learn to let them go and move on to the next level. He never intended for us to be unsure in this life or to be double-minded. To count all joy is not allowing what we go through to control us but rather have control over how we deal with what we go through. It's hard sometimes to count it all joy especially when you're really going through some real hard times.

In July of 2014, my family loss a very influential person suddenly, it was my granny. She was the backbone of our family. I mean we all looked up to her for all the answers pertaining God and life. That's how wise she was. If that wasn't hard enough for me to deal with, in December of that same year, I had to watch my youngest sister pass away. Hers was a sudden death as well.

I was through. Talking about pain and confused, I was like, "God, what in the world is going on?" My whole life kind of went on pause for a while. I didn't know if I could ever recover from those loses. I knew that I had just done, had all I could take, and felt that it was the breaking point in my life. My soul was disturbed. I couldn't think straight, and I most definitely wasn't thinking about counting it all joy. Nope, not at all. As a matter of fact, I was angry at God.

I was like, "Really, God, my granny and my sister." God allowed me the time to grieve. And when I say I vented, I was angry, and God heard about it. I told him all I had been through and how he told me to do something, how I was obedient and did it even when I didn't want to, but because He was who He was in my life—and in life, period—I did it. I cried out, "How dare you take them away like that." I said, "God, my sister had just started to get her life together, and you just take her from us, from her son. How dare you?"

Well needless to say, God wasn't bothered by what I said.

He knew I was hurting. But when He felt I was taking it too far, and I was straying away, He checked me really quick and said, "Okay, enough is enough. Now get up and press on."

I did. And it was hard. I cried most days and noticed that with time, I could look at photos, and it didn't hurt so much or as bad as it once did.

I noticed that eventually I started smiling at the thought of them. Now God had seen me through it all, and I hadn't even realized it. He was working on me and in me and through me. I was able to talk to other people about it and encourage them and tell them that it was going to eventually be okay, that even though it hurt, they would make it through. Why? Because I had made it through.

Here I was again, able to stand and tell people God was able. Wow. I made it through that ordeal, something that I thought was the toughest thing I ever had to do, taking my sister off life support and allowing them to pronounce her legally dead.

What I thought had destroyed me actually, once again, made me stronger. What the enemy meant for my bad God turned a dark situation into a learning experience and a teachable one again. I stay in awe of God constantly in my life. Oh my god, there it is, count it all joy. They aren't suffering here in this world, they are free from the foolishness that we still face today. I elected for my sister to be an organ donor so in my sister's death, others got life. And that was a positive thing I was too distraught to realize as well. No matter the issue, when God sees you, me, or us through, we can count it all joy because we didn't allow those situations to destroy us. Our lives were set up to be living testimonies.

Chapter 6

HIS ARMS ARE
ALWAYS OPEN

What can separate us from the love of God? The Bible tells us nothing can.

More than Conquerors

> What, then, shall we say in response to these things? If God is for us, who can be against us? He who did not spare His own Son but gave Him up for us all— how will He not also, along with Him, graciously give us all things? Who will bring any charge against those whom God has chosen? It is God who justifies. Who then is the one who condemns? No one. Christ Jesus who died—more than that, who was raised to life—is at the

right hand of God and is also interceding for us. Who shall separate us from the
love of Christ? Shall trouble or hardship
or persecution or famine or nakedness or
danger or sword? As it is written:
    "For your sake, we face death all day
long;
    we are considered as sheep to be
slaughtered."
    No, in all these things, we are more
than conquerors through him who loved
us. For I am convinced that neither death
nor life, neither angels nor demons, neither the present nor the future, nor any
powers, neither height nor depth, nor
anything else in all creation, will be able
to separate us from the love of God that
is in Christ Jesus our Lord. (Romans
8:31–39 NIV)

There is nothing that we can do in our lives that can
make God not love us. With this in mind, we need to understand that when we mess up or make a mistake, God will
forgive us when we seek Him in true repentance. The reason why I said true repentance is because God searches the
heart of man/woman, and He knows when we are sincere
and when we are just practicing lip service.

We can fool those around us, and we can even fool ourselves sometimes, but we can never fool God. So that's why
it is always good to be honest with ourselves and with God.
God is looking for a people who are tired of going along to
get along. He is looking for His people to believe that we
are called to be different from the world and to truly know

Who and Whose we are. The Bible says in 2 Chronicles 7:14 (NIV):

> If my people, who are called by my name, will humble themselves and pray and seek my face and turn from their wicked ways, then I will hear from heaven, and I will forgive their sin and will heal their land.

Throughout the Word of God, He keeps telling us all hope isn't lost. I love you all. Repent, and I am faithful to forgive and heal you and/or your situation. What an awesome God we serve! Why then won't we run to the faithful open arms of God? It's because sometime we choose to believe the report of the enemy instead of the report of the Lord. It helps us not to rely on what we feel because we allow our flesh to get in the way of what God is trying to do in our lives.

The enemy will say, "Look at you. You messed up again. there's no turning back now." Well that's a whole lie because God grants us new mercy and grace every day. Each day that we wake up is a new opportunity to do better, to live better, and to be better. There are a hundred reasons to talk yourself out of something that is good for you for your life, but just that one choice to rely on God will change your life forevermore.

I recall an event that happened in the Bible where God's people knew who God was and still was about to talk themselves out of their victory and their blessing. Numbers 13:17–33 (NIV) says:

> When Moses sent them to explore Canaan, he said, "Go up through the Negev and on into the hill country. See

what the land is like and whether the people who live there are strong or weak, few or many. What kind of land do they live in? Is it good or bad? What kind of towns do they live in? Are they unwalled or fortified? How is the soil? Is it fertile or poor? Are there trees in it or not? Do your best to bring back some of the fruit of the land." (It was the season for the first ripe grapes.)

So they went up and explored the land from the Desert of Zin as far as Rehob toward Lebo Hamath. They went up through the Negev and came to Hebron, where Ahiman, Sheshai, and Talmai, the descendants of Anak, lived. (Hebron had been built seven years before Zoan in Egypt.) When they reached the Valley of Eshkol, they cut off a branch bearing a single cluster of grapes. Two of them carried it on a pole between them, along with some pomegranates and figs. That place was called the Valley of Eshkol because of the cluster of grapes the Israelites cut off there. At the end of forty days, they returned from exploring the land.

Report on the Exploration

They came back to Moses and Aaron and the whole Israelite community at Kadesh in the Desert of Paran. There

they reported to them and to the whole
assembly and showed them the fruit of
the land. They gave Moses this account:
"We went into the land to which you sent
us, and it does flow with milk and honey!
Here is its fruit. But the people who live
there are powerful, and the cities are fortified and very large. We even saw descendants of Anak there. The Amalekites live
in the Negev; the Hittites, Jebusites, and
Amorites live in the hill country; and the
Canaanites live near the sea and along the
Jordan." Then Caleb silenced the people
before Moses and said, "We should go
up and take possession of the land, for
we can certainly do it." But the men who
had gone up with him said, "We can't
attack those people. They are stronger
than we are." And they spread among the
Israelites a bad report about the land they
had explored. They said, "The land we
explored devours those living in it. All
the people we saw there are of great size.
We saw the Nephilim there (the descendants of Anak come from the Nephilim).
We seemed like grasshoppers in our own
eyes, and we looked the same to them."

God's people were not new to who He was. By this time,
they knew that they could trust Moses and God at this point,
and yet they chose to come back and have a report contra-
dictive to Whom they belonged to. They had been riding out

with God for a long time, but they chose to believe what they saw instead of in the Mighty God they served.

This excerpt from the Bible isn't something that's in the past. You would think, by reading this thing, it would help us nowadays to learn from our fellow brothers' and sisters' mistakes and do better, right? Wrong. We still look at what we see instead of the God that we say we serve. I remember in 2004, I was trying to finish up my medical assistance course, and it was a struggle. I really didn't know what was about to happen to me in my life.

I had two kids that I was struggling to raise. I was fighting homelessness and trying to work. I was staying with my granny, but she was getting ready to leave and move to Mississippi. I didn't want to go because I was almost done with school, and I wanted to graduated. But if she left, I wouldn't have a place to stay. I just kept pressing and pushing myself all the way up till she got ready to leave. But in between that time, I went through a sexual assault from someone whom I thought was a friend to me.

I was overwhelmed. My heart was heavy. I just wanted to give up on everything. I was burning myself from both ends and trying to deal with what happened to me. And to add to the already horrible situations I was going through, I had found out that I had become pregnant due to the sexual assault that had happened! That was it. I had all I could take. I was through. I was for sure about to throw in the towel.

I had a seven-year-old and a five-year-old counting on me to keep pressing. So I did, with conflict in my heart. What in the world was I going to do? I spoke with my grandmother, and she asked me if I was going to get an abortion, and I said, "Granny, I don't believe in abortions." And she said, "Well all I say is pray and seek God's revelation on what to do in this situation".

She eventually left, and I was left on my own, so I asked my son's grandmother to let me stay until I finished school, and she said yes, so I did. But the baby kept growing, and I kept feeling sad, hurt, and confused. I cried out to the Lord, "Please help me. I don't know what to do. This is way too much on my plate. My son's grandmother knew my struggle, and she suggested an abortion and offered to pay for it. She told me that if I got the abortion that I could just live with her until I got on my feet. But if I kept the child, I had to find somewhere else to live because she was getting older and couldn't do the whole baby crying thing.

She asked for an answer the next day, so I went to sleep with a heavy burden in my spirit. To tell the truth, I didn't want or need another child, especially not now in my life with all that I was going through. I remember that night, I had a dream of walking in this beautiful place—a forest of some sort—and I was at peace without a care in the world there.

I heard a voice speak to me and said, "Candice do not abort this child. If you have this child, I promise to take care of this child and you, and neither of you shall worry about homelessness again. I woke up the next morning and talked to her and told her that I was going to keep the baby.

She said, "Are you sure?"

I said, "Yes. I believe God spoke to me and wants me to keep the baby."

She said, "So you are going to allow your religious belief to make this decision for you?"

I said, "Yes, ma'am."

She said, "Well okay, you know what you have to do."

I said, "Yes, ma'am."

I finished school and my clinical. So now I had to find a place to go. I called my oldest sister who was living in

Wisconsin at the time and told her my situation, and she told me I could come there.

I asked my granny's sister to come and drive me and my son to Wisconsin. We moved in with my sister who, after the baby was born, placed me in a shelter.

Okay, what's going on, God?

It was October when You spoke those words to me. I moved to Wisconsin in November. And here I was, February, and I was homeless again, going back into a shelter.

Could this mean that maybe I didn't hear from God like I thought I did? Could I have just made the biggest mistake of my life and added more on me than I could handle?

What is going on, God?

Then I heard, "Trust Me."

So I went through the process, and I was hurt and disappointed and scared and broken. Mind you, I still had a five-year-old that I had to fight for to get back. But how, if I couldn't ever get out of this homelessness?

As soon as I started to do things to help myself, things just started to fall in place for me. I began to see that in all I did, I had favor. Everything just simply went my way. The program I was in was a thirty-day program. Sadly, at the end of my thirty days, I was not ready to move out. But on the thirty-third day of the program, I had keys to my own apartment.

Look at God. Why don't you! Not only did I get the place, but people furnished my whole apartment, baby crib, and all. I had dishes, cleaning supplies, and people brought groceries. I had more than enough of everything. I was in my place for two weeks, and people were still showing up. I had to tell them that I had all I needed and to please help others because I was good.

That was fourteen years ago, and I have been on my feet since then. And guess what, God did just what He said. He has proved to me, time and time again, that I can trust Him, and that no matter what, His arms are always open.

Chapter 7

HE'S AN ON-TIME GOD

He's an on-time God. Yes, He is an on-time God, yes, he is. Job said that He may not come when you want Him, but He is always right on time. Now how many have heard someone sing this or heard it playing at some point in your life? Some may wonder now just what does this really mean.

Have you ever been in a situation in your life where you may have been going through something really difficult, and you were wondering, *God, how long must I endure this suffering?* All of us have gone through this as a follower of Jesus or not. We have all wondered how long we would be stuck in a situation that seemed as if it had no resolution, a situation that totally shook the very foundation we were on.

What do you do when you are faced with situations such as this? Well let's see what the Word of God has to say about what we need to know.

Wait on the Lord: be of good courage, and He shall strengthen thine heart: wait, I say, on the Lord. (Psalm 27:14 KJV)

But they that wait upon the Lord shall renew their strength; they shall mount up with wings as eagles; they shall run and not be weary; and they shall walk and not faint. (Isaiah 40:31 KJV)

I waited patiently for the Lord; He turned to me and heard my cry. He lifted me out of the slimy pit, out of the mud and mire; He set my feet on a rock and gave me a firm place to stand. He put a new song in my mouth, a hymn of praise to our God. Many will see and fear the Lord and put their trust in Him. Blessed is the one who trusts in the Lord, who does not look to the proud, to those who turn aside to false gods. (Psalm 40:1–4 NIV)

Dear friends, don't ignore this fact: One day with the Lord is like a thousand years, and a thousand years are like one day. The Lord isn't slow to do what he promised as some people think. Rather he is patient for your sake. He doesn't want to destroy anyone but wants all people to have an opportunity to turn to Him and change the way they think and act. (2 Peter 3:8–9 GW)

These scriptures are meant to show us that we are not alone. Yes, others have gone through hardships, and they too survived, and they trusted in God and waited on His perfect timing and came to see that He is most definitely on time God. He doesn't see things the way that we do. He knows our beginning before our end and knows what we can handle even when we don't. That's why we have to trust Him. Who then can we trust for guidance if not for God, the Creator of the world, the stars, the galaxies?

I remember crying to my granny over the phone about some issues. And interestingly enough, she would always ask me, "Well did you pray about it?" I would say yes, and she would say, "Then why are you still talking about it?" She would say, "If you are going to pray about something, then you have to trust in the power of the One that you are praying to."

She would say, "Candice, ain't nobody tell you this world, or your walk with God, was going to be easy. Jesus went through. So guess what you are going to go through too. Hard times will come. You just have to be strong and endure. Troubles don't last always. Those were wise words from a beautiful soul. I treasured each conversation I had with my grandmother. She was our elder, and it always paid off listening to her advice.

I know waiting on God or anyone else is something that most of us have a hard time with especially since we live in the age of right now. If you need to know something, it's right at the tip of your finger. Technology has made us impatient and lazy. You really don't have to wait too long in this world we live in. But when it comes to God, He doesn't go by the standards of this world. He is the I am God and do things the way He sees fit and the way He knows will benefit us the most.

He knows that sometimes it's not good for things to be rushed. He knows that if we go through something too fast, we may miss the most important things. *He* works on His timing because His timing is the right timing, no matter what we think or how we may feel about it.

We don't know our future, so therefore we don't know the things that lay before us. We can't see those things that can potentially cause us hurt, harm, and danger, and rushing into something can cause catastrophic results. Think about it, would you want a surgeon to rush through school, not collecting all the wisdom and knowledge he needs from school to be a competent surgeon?

Would you want your cardiologist to rush through your heart surgery? Of course not. You would want him to take his time to make sure that he is efficient in what he is doing. Why then would you want to rush through this life, not fully knowing what lies ahead of you? It would be best to seek the Creator and wait on Him to lead you and guide you through this life because He is all-seeing and all-knowing.

He got this, and He has you and me. We can trust that waiting on Him, we will be okay. Waiting is no fun. While we wait, we can keep busy doing things that we know God wants, like searching His Word, having praise and worship, praying, helping, and being there for others while we wait. And before you know it, you will have overcome those things in which you were struggling with.

You will see that He will be done, made a way right before your eyes. He has a habit of doing that. While you are busy helping seeing others through, He will be done worked it all out for you. And by the time you realize what He has done, you will have forgotten about the issue. You take a step back and say with surety, "Look at You, God, you have done it again. You just made a way for me again." The point of trusting Him is to take a back seat and allow God to be God. One of my favorite worship songs is a song by Marvin Sapp called "Praise Him in Advance." When we have faith and trust in the God that we serve, we can give Him praise in advance for the breakthrough, for the miracle, for the healing, or whatever it is that you may be seeking Him for. Stand tall, be firm, and keep pressing your way through. We must never give up, and we must never give in, because through Jesus, God has made sure that no matter what it is that we face in this life that we win, that we are victorious. Whose report are you willing to believe? Are you going to listen to the naysayers, or are you going to believe the Word of God that says in Romans 8:37 (NIV), "No, in all these things, we are more than conquerors through Him who loved us"?

He made us the head and not the tail. He created us to be above our circumstances and not beneath them. He created us to have dominion over the earth. Yes, the devil is down here, reaping havoc all over the earth, and it seems as if the above statement is a lie. Well I am here to let you know, it is a fact. The sooner the people of God start to realize we are (we exist) because He *is* (who He is in our lives and for our lives), the better off we will all be and the more we will start to see the move of God in our lives daily.

Chapter 8

NOT TODAY, SATAN

I have heard people say that every time something crazy or something bad happens to them in their lives, they would say, "Okay now, not today, Satan." I have heard people use that phrase in a joking way. And I have heard people use it with conviction, and they truly mean it with every fiber of their being.

Those who say it with conviction are those of us who can see the enemy at a start point of mess and foolery, and we decide to nip his foolery in the bud before it gets blown out and become a huge issue. I know that I have said it a lot in my life so much, so my children started to mimic me, not fully understanding what I was saying it for. So I would take opportunities like that as teachable moments for my children.

I would ask them questions, and they would answer them. And I would always remind them that their spirituality was not a game. It was their lifeline and should be taken very seriously. This is something I don't play with. Have I? Yes, I have, but it was before I knew not to. Sometimes we do things and think, no harm, no foul. But God is not a toy or a game to be played with for our amusement.

He is the great I am, and we all must understand that and always show God the respect that is due to Him at all times. We all slip up, and we all sin and fall short of God's glory. But when we know better, we ought to do better.

We are the example that our children see. It is our jobs as stewards over their lives to raise them to have a reverent fear of the Lord. So if they see us not being genuine with God, neither will they. I recall when my husband had an issue with alcohol, and he would be sort of a mean drunk. One day he decided that he would go on a drinking binge, and I told him that he had to stop because, well, he was ruing our relationship. He listened to me, and he tried to stop and was doing good for some time. But how many of you know that when you are trying to do right, the enemy will come in and say, "Oops, you thought you had that under control." Well he fell and decided to take a drive. I tried to stop him. And in the midst of the argument, I heard the Lord speak to me and tell me to let him go, so I did. I was concerned for Him, but I had to be obedient. I was in the kitchen cooking when I got a call from his mother. She was concerned, and she asked me if he had been drinking and where he was. I simply told her yes and that he wasn't there, and we hung up. I heard the Lord say, "Pray for your husband now, and I did. I didn't know what to pray for, so I just started, and the spirit took over. I was praying for what seemed like an hour. But it was actually about fifteen or thirty minutes. I heard, "Call your husband," so I did. But he didn't answer. Then a few moments later, I got a call from him, and he said, "Baby, I was just in a wreck, but I am okay."

I said, "What did you just say?"

He said, "I just wrecked the truck, but I'm okay."

I was in total and complete shock. When he got home, he told me he couldn't tell how the accident even happened. He said there weren't even any cars around him at the time. He said that it was raining, and something popped at the back tire, and he lost control and ran off the road. He said he tried to control the car but couldn't. All he could do was let it happen and pray. The truck hit some trees going down until it finally stopped. He told me that when he was hitting the trees, he felt as if something was holding him and shielding him. He walked away with just a whiplash. He said he couldn't say anything but that he knew it had been God that spared his life that day, especially how the truck was so smashed. I got goose bumps that day. And as I was writing these words, I was getting them. Because the moment God spoke in my spirit to pray for my husband, this accident was about to take place. And as I was being obedient, he too was praying. And the Word of God says in Matthew 18:20 (NIV): "For where two or three gather in my name, there am I with them." The two of us were praying, and God showed up and showed out that day. And what the enemy meant for bad God turned that whole situation all around, and it changed my husband that day. His relationship strengthened with the Lord that day. And God showed me, one more time, that He was God, and how awesome His might and His power was. He showed me that He is always there, working on behalf of His child. And as we are obedient to His will, His Word, and His way, things will turn out good for those of us that love the Lord our God.

"And we know that in all things, God works for the good of those who love him, who have been called according to his purpose" (Romans 8:28 NIV). I knew then, and I know now, that we have the power through the Holy Spirit to say, "Oh no, not today, Satan." I know that you too may have this testimony in your life if you just look back over your life and see where God has showed up and turned it all around for you. You don't have to, I don't have to, we don't have to allow the enemy to come into our lives and reap havoc. We have the power to control what goes on with us and those things that we can't deal with on our own. All we have to do is just turn it over to the Holy Trinity. Keep in mind the Serenity Prayer. I am sure most of us grew up with this prayer in the home:

Serenity Prayer by Reinhold Niebuhr (1892–1971)

> God, grant me the serenity to accept the things I cannot change, courage to change the things I can, and wisdom to know the difference; living one day at a time; enjoying one moment at a time; accepting hardships as the pathway to peace; taking, as He did, this sinful world as it is, not as I would have it; trusting that He will make all things right if I surrender to His will; that I may be reasonably happy in this life and supremely happy with Him forever in the next. Amen.

This is a prayer that has helped me with so much over the years, as well as the Lord's Prayer, which states in Matthew 6:9–13 (KJV):

> After this manner, therefore pray ye: Our Father, which art in heaven, hallowed be Thy name. Thy kingdom come, Thy will be done in earth as it is in heaven. Give us

this day our daily bread. And forgive us
our debts as we forgive our debtors. And
lead us not into temptation but deliver us
from evil: For Thine is the kingdom, and
the power, and the glory, forever. Amen.

God set it up for us to have that escape that we need to
flea temptation. He made it so we know that there is nothing
that can hold us back in life but us. We can go to the Bible
and find inspiration for just about anything. The enemy will
trick you and have you thinking you aren't going to make it
or be anything in this life. And if you don't know the Word
of God, he will succeed in doing so. The Word of Gods says
in Romans 8 (KJV):

There is therefore now no condemna-
tion to them, which are in Christ Jesus
who walk not after the flesh but after the
Spirit.

It's all there. All the motivation, all the wisdom, all the
knowledge you need are right there in the Word of God.
That's why He specified that we study to show ourselves
approved, to read the Word, to study the Word, to meditate
on the Word day and night, and to pray without ceasing.
Because what He was and is trying to do is to get His people
ready to be strong for the task ahead of all of us individually,
as well as collectively. We all were created for a purpose and a
plan. And God will prefect His plan through us but only as
we allow Him to do so. It's time to stand up for ourselves and
say with a mighty boldness—not today, Satan!

Chapter 9

MORE THAN ENOUGH

We were not all born with silver spoons in our mouths. I am one of those that wasn't. I remember one time as a child, we stayed in a building that was above a store in Chicago on the south side. We would always go to the store almost every day, so the owner knew us. My mother and stepfather struggled a lot as a young married couple, but they tried to hide it as much as they could from us. There were times when it was hard for them to do it.

We were without food and without electricity. My mother didn't want to bother her parents, and my stepdad didn't want to go to his family because they didn't approve and/or like my mother. We went without lights and food for a while. I remember seeing my mom sitting in a chair one time, praying. She was crying and praying, and she heard a knock at the door.

She got up and answered the door, and it was the mail guy, and he handed her a piece of mail. She looked down at that piece of mail and started shouting for joy and saying, "Thank you, Jesus."

I was like, "Mom, what's wrong?"

She said, "Nothing, baby. God answered my prayers. I just received some unexpected money in the mail. Now we can eat and have lights."

God has a way about Him that just when you think you are counted out or that this is the end, He sends help. And when you receive the help, it covers that issue and more.

I recall the story of the widow in the Bible in 2 Kings 4:1–7 (NIV).

The Widow's Olive Oil

> The wife of a man from the company of the prophets cried out to Elisha, "Your servant, my husband, is dead, and you know that he revered the Lord. But now his creditor is coming to take my two boys as his slaves." Elisha replied to her, "How can I help you? Tell me, what do you have in your house?" "Your servant has nothing there at all," she said, "except a small jar of olive oil." Elisha said, "Go around and ask all your neighbors for empty jars. Don't ask for just a few. Then go inside and shut the door behind you and your sons. Pour oil into all the jars, and as each is filled, put it to one side." She left him and shut the door behind her and her sons. They brought the jars

to her and she kept pouring. When all
the jars were full, she said to her son,
"Bring me another one." But he replied,
"There is not a jar left." Then the oil
stopped flowing. She went and told the
man of God, and he said, "Go, sell the
oil and pay your debts. You and your sons
can live on what is left."

When I read this in the Bible, it reminded me of so
many times, growing up, that things like this happened for
my mother and/or grandmother. And as I grew up, I have
seen it happen to me. It's interesting how the Lord our God
works. He will allow us to exhaust all our own avenues when
we refuse to come to Him first.

He will let us see for ourselves that He is absolutely all
that we need and more. I am also reminded of a few more
times God had showed us who He is and what He can do.
Let's look at when he fed the five thousand men, not including the women and children that were there. So it was, in all
actuality, more than five thousand.

Jesus Feeds the Five Thousand

When Jesus heard what had happened,
He withdrew by boat privately to a sol-
itary place. Hearing of this, the crowds
followed Him on foot from the towns.
When Jesus landed and saw a large crowd,
He had compassion on them and healed
their sick. As evening approached, the
disciples came to Him and said, "This
is a remote place, and it's already getting

late. Send the crowds away so they can go to the villages and buy themselves some food." Jesus replied, "They do not need to go away. You give them something to eat." "We have here only five loaves of bread and two fish," they answered.

"Bring them here to Me," He said. And He directed the people to sit down on the grass. Taking the five loaves and the two fish and looking up to heaven, He gave thanks and broke the loaves. Then he gave them to the disciples, and the disciples gave them to the people. They all ate and were satisfied, and the disciples picked up twelve basketfuls of broken pieces that were leftover. The number of those who ate was about five thousand men, besides women and children. (Matthew 14:13–21 NIV)

God keep showing us His greatness. He keeps showing us time and time again that we can always trust Him to be the provider He says that He is in His word. He shows us that He can provide and do it exceedingly, abundantly, above all we can ever ask for. He is known for being the more-than-enough God. Throughout life, He has shown Himself to you, to me, to us in some kind of way, whether we realize it at the time or not. The Word of God tells us in Psalm 34:8 (KJV):

O, taste and see that the Lord is good: blessed is the man that trusteth in him.

The Amplified version says in Psalm 34:8:

> O, taste and see that the Lord (our God)
> is good; how blessed (fortunate, prosper-
> ous, and favored by God) is the man who
> takes refuge in Him.

As we take our trust out of our own ability to do things and the ability of others to do for us, we begin to see the Lord our God for who He is. And who He is and has always been more than enough. I remember when my two oldest were older, I decided I would finish my education. I was seventeen when I had my son and nineteen when I had my daughter, so I didn't get a chance to finish school. I got a job to take care of us. In 2002, I said I needed to get a better job. Minimum wage just wasn't cutting it for a mother with two kids even then.

I contacted Triton College in River Grove, Illinois, and signed up to take the test. When the time came to take the test, I was nervous because I hadn't been to school in a while. I prayed and prayed and told the Lord He had to see me through this because I didn't know if I would be able to do it.

I got there and went on the elevator. And this lady got on with me, and she asked me where I was headed. I looked upset. I said I was going to take my GED, and she looked at me and said, "Oh, you are going to pass it with flying colors," and smiled, and I went off. I said one more prayer and took the test.

A few weeks later, I got a letter in the mail telling me not only did I pass, but I scored the max on everything. And when I tell you I shouted, I shouted and thanked God for doing what only He could in my life. I went on to get my certified nursing assistant certification. And from there, I went to get my medical assistance certification. And later on, I went to business school and school for psychology. God had seen me through it all.

I have learned that God is faithful and will do what He says. I have never been disappointed with Him at all in my life because He is the only faithful presence that's been there for me. When my mother failed me and let me down, He was there. When my so-called friends failed, used, and abused me, He was there. He has been there picking up all the broken pieces of my life and putting them back together again but not the way I was before but making sure that I was better than I was before.

When God allows things to transpire in our lives, it's never to cause us hurt, harm, or danger. It is strictly to make us stronger, wiser, and braver than we were when we started out. I remember, before I realized God's hand at work in my life, I would wonder what it was that I did that was so bad in my life that I would always go through such heartache.

Why did this happen? Why did that happen? I had no control over a majority of the things that happened. But then there were the things that transpired through the poor decisions I made through being unknowledgeable about life. I had the whole woe in me down packed.

One day while in one of my seasons of self-loath and self-pity, I heard in my spirit, "Without the tests, you wouldn't have the testimonies. And without the trials, you would not have the triumphs. You thinking this is all about you. It's not. What you make it through will help to see others through. Now get up and keep pressing. You have work yet to do."

Things like this spoken to me have kept me over the years to keep moving when I just really felt like giving up. No one really wants to suffer especially not for strangers.

Well Jesus did it. He suffered and was crucified for people He knew weren't all going to appreciate His sacrifice.

He did it for the few of us that He saw promise in, for those of us He knew would try and press and keep pressing and trying and believing. He went above and beyond for you and for me. He has always done more than enough in the lives of all believers.

Chapter 10

CHANGE ME, LORD

To Know the Lord, our God, is to love Him. Why then do we love God? The Word of God says in 1 John 4:19 (KJV):

We love Him because He first loved us.

I have learned that as I read, the Word God revealed to me those things that I needed work on. He knows we all have fault and flaws, and He enables us to invoke the change that we need through His Word and through the power and the anointing of His Holy Spirit. We are to obtain wisdom to apply to our daily lives and to help others around us.

A couple of years ago, I started a Bible study with a few friends of mine because I wanted to share with them the things that was helping me to grow. And I wanted to learn from them as well. Every Saturday, the Spirit would show up, and it was always awesome. We felt growth from all those things we learned each week, and we applied it to our lives, using it wherever we went and seen an opportunity to witness.

Whether it was at work or the doctor's office or even to our families, we would try to reach one and teach those things that we learned and felt growth from. This is the task of all the children of God. Like the song says, I pray for you, and you pray for me. I need you to survive. We all need each other. And God use people to bless other people.

Reading the Word and applying it to your life should provoke change. There should be some kind of evidence that change is taking place in our lives. Our character should be changing how we deal with life. And the people in it should begin to change. You have to, I have to, we have to do our part and live the Word that we are reading so those who are thirsty for God will see the light of God in us, and we can lead them to Him.

The Word says in Matthew 5:16 (KJV):

> Let your light to shine before men that
> they may see your good works and glorify
> your Father which is in heaven.

We have to change. We have to grow as children of God. We should not allow ourselves to become complacent with the way we are. There should be a fire burning on the inside of us that we don't want extinguished. There should be a thirst for more of God and His wisdom and His power.

We ought to always be ready and willing to go forward and move higher in the Lord. Every day I ask God to change me. Why? Because the way that I was wasn't working out good for me. I tried to handle this thing called life by myself. I just couldn't do it. I had no real guidance, and I kept allowing the wrong people in my life. I had no insight. I had no discernment.

When I decided to give up trying to do it all myself and seek the Lord first before I did things, I begin to see a change—a wonderful change—in my life. People that I thought were meant to be in my life left me. It got to the point that the only people I had in my life were my kids and God. But let me tell you, I didn't feel lonely, or like I was missing out on something.

I got in the Word and read and studied and went to church and worked. God was changing me from the inside out, and change was taking place in me that I didn't even know was taking place. I just looked around one day and saw God had isolated me to do a work on me and in me so He could work through me.

This is a stage that most people can successfully make it through because they feel like they just have to have people around them. And most people don't even care who the people are, just as long as there are people around so they don't have to be alone. This is a process that is necessary for change to take place.

God has to strip you away from people and things that are no good for you so that you can be filled up with the things that you need for your purpose. And He will send people—the right people—in your life at the right time to help you with things that you need in your life according to His purpose for your life and the lives of those that He is going to send along your path for you to help.

He knew that you need, I need, we need this change to take place not only to help ourselves but also to help other people. Change is not optional in this life. It is necessary for the children of God for our growth mentally, emotionally, physically, and spiritually.

Why is change so important? Well I'm glad you asked. It's important because when God comes into your life and has called you for any reason, we see that He is so great and different. We too have to be different from the people in this world. To know God and to love Him is to change and to know that this change pleases Him.

As the children of God, we are ambassadors of the kingdom of God, and we have to be the example the world sees. So if we give our life to the Lord, our God, and don't allow change to take place, we are no different than the people in the world. And that can't be, because the Word of God says in Matthew 15:16–20 (NIV):

> "Are you still so dull?" Jesus asked them. "Don't you see that whatever enters the mouth goes into the stomach and then out of the body? But the things that come out of a person's mouth come from the heart, and these defile them.
>
> For out of the heart come evil thoughts—murder, adultery, sexual immorality, theft, false testimony, slander. These are what defile a person. But eating with unwashed hands does not defile them."

He was saying that change starts in the heart of man, for from the heart, their actions flow—good or bad. It is up to us to accept change to live a better life. Once again, change is not easy, but it is necessary. It's not going to always be what you want or desire, but it is what you need.

I will not lie to you and tell you, "Oh well, God has changed me, and I have it all together," because I don't. I am still growing daily, and God is continuously working on me. God doesn't want us to ignore the change that we need.

Instead He asks that we embrace the change and trust Him to see us through the process. He is more than capable of doing it, and it pleases Him to do so. He also doesn't want us to pretend like we have changed. I remember in the Bible how Pharaoh tried to pretend, and it didn't work very well for him. The Word of God says in Exodus 9:27–34 (NIV):

> Then Pharaoh summoned Moses and Aaron. "This time I have sinned," he said to them. "The Lord is in the right, and I and my people are in the wrong. Pray to the Lord, for we have had enough thunder and hail. I will let you go. You don't have to stay any longer." Moses replied, "When I have gone out of the city, I will spread out my hands in prayer to the Lord. The thunder will stop, and there will be no more hail, so you may know that the earth is the Lord's. But I know that you and your officials still do not fear the Lord God."
>
> (The flax and barley were destroyed, since the barley had headed and the flax was in bloom. The wheat and spelt, however, were not destroyed because they ripen later.) Then Moses left Pharaoh and went out of the city. He spread out his hands toward the Lord. The thunder and hail stopped, and the rain no longer poured down on the land. When Pharaoh saw that the rain and hail and thunder had stopped, he sinned again: He and his officials hardened their hearts.

We can't try to manipulate God and pretend God knows all and sees all and is the reader of man's heart, so He knows if we are genuine or not. My granny used to say, "Girl, you can fool people some of the time, but you can fool God none of the time because He created you, and He knows you."

We can put on a nice show for people and pretend like we have changed, but we can only do that for so long before our true nature begins to resurface, and people will see that we were just pretending to be something or someone we are not. This is why we must all be true for change to take place and manifest in our lives.

Chapter 11

COMMUNICATION IS A KEY

There are many keys that unlock life's doors to greater and better things, and communication is one of them. As a child of the Most High God, there should never be a time when we are not in constant communication with God. Even when we are feeling our worst, we need to press through all that and still come to the Lord, our God, in prayer, praise, and worship.

We can't allow anything or anyone to knock us off our square or to hold us back. Jesus's purpose wasn't to come and heal people and show miracles, signs, and wonders. His purpose was to come here and die and be resurrected for mankind, for a sinful world and a sinful people that we may be able to ask for forgiveness and be in communication with God for ourselves through our relationship with Jesus.

How then can we communicate with God and/or the Holy Trinity? Good, I'm glad that you asked. Well it's through prayer, meditating on His word and praise and worship. God speaks to the heart of man. And the only way to hear Him, you have to have an open heart and a listening spiritual ear to hear what the spirit of the Lord is saying, being careful to make sure that you are answering only to the voice of the Lord and not the temptation of the enemy.

We can talk to the Lord, our God, anytime we want to, wherever we want to, because there is no place that we can go that God doesn't know where we are. In order to work in our full capacity, we will need a right relationship with God. We have to stay focused on what we know we are supposed to be doing and less on what people around us are or aren't doing.

We need to stay in our own lane and do what the Lord says pertaining to our own lives, unless we are told otherwise. Because moving too fast to talk to people who aren't ready to hear or ready to receive a word from God can cause some spiritual damage to people. We need to stay in communication with God so we can know when to move and when not to move.

Communicating with God will let us know when it is time to move up in life or to move on in this life. When God is speaking, we have to pay attention because he uses places, people, even signs to speak to us. So we are to always be focused on God and what He is telling us.

How many times can you recall when you were getting ready to go somewhere, and you heard in your spirit, "Wait," and you did, and that spared your life? I remember a time when my husband and I were on our way to Mississippi to see about my mom, and I wanted to leave at a particular time, but I just couldn't get out the door. Everything came up and kept setting my time back. I finally got on the highway almost an hour later, then we got stuck in traffic that wasn't supposed to be there.

We got up through there and saw that there had been a car accident, really bad. Cars piled up. I just said, before I knew it, I said, "God, thank you." And then I said, "Please be with them."

I said thank you to God at that moment because at that exact moment, I knew why I was being held back because that would have been me if I had left at the time I was planning to.

When you are in constant communication with God, it can save your life. God is with me in all that I go through. He is with all His people. No matter what the situation or issue is, He is there. And it is through our relationship with God that we can be sure that He is and will always be there for all His people.

God has a way of reaching out and speaking to us that may seem unnatural and not normal or out of the ordinary. But it is through this that God tests our obedience, and we get to see that we are truly interacting with the Lord, our God. God will give us the information that we need all the time to go forth and do His will.

We have to establish a trust between God and ourselves. In doing so in establishing this trust, we will see that God doesn't need us to always know everything all at once. We just need to be obedient. Focus on God, and listen to God and the information that is taking place as we communicate with Him. We can be assured that he is trustworthy and that He will never leave nor forsake His people. Whatever it is that God has called us to do, He will sustain us to be able to do it.

He works with the impossible and wants us to know that there is nothing too hard for Him, and that with Him, all things are possible. We have to trust God, and God has to be able to count on and trust us to listen and do exactly what

He says at all times, not when we feel like doing it. We don't have time to let people who are not trying to see us do better or be better to have a say in our lives.

People will try to tear you down while God is trying to build you up. I recall times that my husband, Terrance, and I were going through real tough times in our marriage. The enemy was trying to destroy the covenant that God had ordained, and it almost worked. But I kept listening to the Lord.

He would tell me, "No, don't say that" or "don't do that" or "listen to Terrance and just be silent." There were even times when the Lord told me to fall back and let him deal with the situation. And I did. And He did what only He could do for me, my husband, and our marriage. I was talking to the wrong people.

I was talking to people. And God wanted me to only talk to Him about what I was going through, because the people I was talking to did not have the wisdom that I needed to help my situation. They were going through their own marital situations and didn't know what to do for themselves. So the best thing for me to do was listen to the source of everything to save the marriage that He ordained.

I was told by others to leave my husband and to divorce him, that he wasn't ever going to change. But God! I listened to God's report and instructions, and here he and I are, still together, better than we were when we started, all because we chose to listen to God instead of allowing people to ruin a beautiful thing.

The enemy will try to destroy everything that God placed in your life to build you. And if you are not in constant communication, and if you don't have a personal relationship with God, you will be defeated, and Satan will win.

71

Allowing the enemy to win is never good, especially when the Word tells us that we are victorious.

We can't be defeated and victorious at the same time. We have to pick one, and hopefully, we all choose to be victorious. The enemy will use people to come into your life and bring you a false sense of reality to distract you from hearing from God. That is why you have to be very careful who you associate with. The wrong associations will become a hindrance and a blockage in your communicating with God the way you need to.

As I write these words, I am reminded of the story of Cain and Abel. The word says in Genesis 4:1–16 (NIV):

Cain and Abel

> Adam made love to his wife, Eve, and she became pregnant and gave birth to Cain. She said, "With the help of the Lord, I have brought forth a man." Later she gave birth to his brother Abel.
>
> Now Abel kept flocks, and Cain worked the soil. In the course of time, Cain brought some of the fruits of the soil as an offering to the Lord. And Abel also brought an offering—fat portions from some of the firstborn of his flock. The Lord looked with favor on Abel and his offering, but on Cain and his offering, he did not look with favor. So Cain was very angry, and his face was downcast. Then the Lord said to Cain, "Why are you angry? Why is your face downcast? If you do what is right, will you not

be accepted? But if you do not do what is right, sin is crouching at your door. It desires to have you, but you must rule over it." Now Cain said to his brother Abel, "Let's go out to the field." While they were in the field, Cain attacked his brother Abel and killed him. Then the Lord said to Cain, "Where is your brother Abel?"

"I don't know," he replied. "Am I my brother's keeper?"

The Lord said, "What have you done? Listen! Your brother's blood cries out to me from the ground. Now you are under a curse and driven from the ground, which opened its mouth to receive your brother's blood from your hand. When you work the ground, it will no longer yield its crops for you. You will be a restless wanderer on the earth."

Cain said to the Lord, "My punishment is more than I can bear. Today you are driving me from the land, and I will be hidden from your presence; I will be a restless wanderer on the earth, and whoever finds me will kill me." But the Lord said to him, "Not so, anyone who kills Cain will suffer vengeance seven times over." Then the Lord put a mark on Cain so that no one who found him would kill him. So Cain went out from the Lord's presence and lived in the land of Nod, east of Eden.

To me, this was utterly ridiculous. Cain, through his laziness and his jealousy of his brother's relationship with God, murdered his brother and became the first murderer. All this could have been prevented if he did what Abel did and established a relationship of respect and communication with God. We don't have to be envious of how others are being blessed by God when we can have our own relationship with Him and have that open line of communication we all need with Him to survive.

Chapter 12

It's Just a Mirage

What is a mirage? The word is defined as an unrealistic hope or wish that cannot be achieved. A mirage is something that appears real or possible but is not in fact so. This is the whole plan and the plot of the enemy in the lives of the believer. He wants to get us to a point where we are so hurt or so mad and or frustrated with God and this journey in life so he can slip right in and try to sell us a mirage.

It will seem so much like the real deal until that moment you sense something is not quite right, and you start to investigate and see that you have fallen for another of the enemy's traps. In 1998, I met my daughter's father. I had Nashowa already, my oldest son, and I was just trying to be the best mom I could be. I was trying to raise him as a single mother, and God knew I needed help.

His grandmother was there. But what I wanted was his father to be there and to help me raise our son. I was desperate for my child to have his father in his life. So much so, I ended up proposing to him for Father's Day that year. That was the most crushing moment for me. All I wanted was our little family to work, but he told me, "Absolutely not," and it crushed me so bad I left feeling defeated.

These are the type of things and feelings that the enemy will be looking for so he can step in and set up his mirages. I left that night, headed back to my mother's house because I had to work the next morning. I made it to Forest Park "L" station, and surprisingly that night, there wasn't a cab in sight. So I waited and waited—still nothing.

Another train had come with some more passengers, and down came John, my daughter's father. He was an older guy, and he came and sat right by me. I was not paying him any attention. I had just got my little heart broken, and I was tired and needed to get home. He started to talk to me. At first I ignored him but then talked to him to pass the time while we waited for a cab. He told me a lot about himself and his life, and mostly I just listened.

He asked me what was I doing out this time of the night with such a young child, and I told him I was coming from my sister's house in Chicago. Then a nurse stopped by us in an all-white uniform and said, "Aw, what a cute family." I looked like, "I don't know this man," and he looked at me and laughed. Then a cab finally showed up, and he went to talk to the cab to ask if we could share the cab. The driver said yes, and he got dropped off first, left his number with me, and told me to call him.

I took his number, and the driver took me home. A few days to a week later, I was cleaning out my wallet. And here the number was. I was about to throw it in the trash but had a feeling not to. So I called him and left a message for him to call me back, and he did. And I would like to say that that was the start of a beautiful romance. But it wasn't. It was the beginning of a long twelve-year nightmare that ended with him almost taking my life. Just like God knows what we desire, well so does the enemy. And the difference with God and the enemy giving us the desires of our hearts is when the Lord adds something or someone to your life, they are there to help you and bless you.

When the enemy sends someone into your life, he sends them there to distract you from your destiny and your purpose and to destroy you. The enemy used my kid's dad and sent him into my life as a mirage, something appearing to be what I needed, but it wasn't. I was nineteen when I met him, and he was twenty-nine and a heroin addict, which I learned this and so many other bad things about him and his family after I got pregnant with my daughter.

I suffered abuse from him and his family, and so did our daughter after she was born. He made all these promises to be there for me and the kids and ended up going to prison for the first five years of our daughter's life, which left me to fend for myself now with two kids. It was a snowball of events that happened that was horrific.

See, when the enemy gets a foot in the door in your life, he comes in after that and reaps havoc in. And by the time he and his demons are done with you and your life, if you are not dead or strung out on drugs or in a mental institution, you somehow wish you were.

During this period of my life, I was a praying woman. I faced obstacles everywhere I turned. Those where the worst years of my life. But if it had not been for those times, I would have never been able to have the relationship that I have with the Holy Trinity. God had to literally come in and intervene to save my life, to save my sanity.

It took prayer, deliverance, and fasting to get me out the deep hole the enemy had me in. I got to see the enemy at work in my life, and I got to see the hand of God and His mercy in my life. When I tell y'all that if it had not been for the Lord who was on my side, I would be dead, I am not kidding.

God has spared my life so many times. Every time I would think I was safe, the enemy would send another mirage and another, until I cried out to the Lord and said, "God, please help me. I'm tired of this. Reveal to me the enemy in my life. Give me the spirit of discernment. I want to see him and his attack so I can be prepared."

How many of y'all know that when you ask God for something, He will give it to you. I was not ready for what I was asking for. I did not know what I was asking for. But I was able to see, and I would pray and pray, and things began to change for me for the better. The enemy wasn't able to get me so easily. I saw him coming and prayed my way through.

The enemy doesn't care if you are young or old, or rather you are a good or bad person. His whole tactic is to kill, steal, and destroy. He preys on the weak, on the ignorant, and on the gullible people in the world. Why? Because they are an easy target. He attacks the strong and faithful to God too. Look at what he did to Job.

He attacks the strong-minded and the faithful. He just knows he has to come with all he has with them because that is a real battle. We have to always be on the lookout for the fake people that are in our lives sent as mirages by the enemy so that he can get a foot in the door. How then can we prevent this from happening?

I will tell you this that you might not always be able to see him for who he is at first because he is good at what he does. The Word of God says in 1 Peter 5:7–9 (GNT):

> Leave all your worries with him because
> he cares for you. Be alert, be on watch!
> Your enemy, the devil, roams around like

a roaring lion, looking for someone to devour. Be firm in your faith, and resist him, because you know that other believers in all the world are going through the same kind of sufferings.

God's Word is filled with warnings and parables about the devil. But it also tells us that God is there and will always be there for his children. Jesus said that he is the Good Shepherd.

The thief comes only to steal and kill and destroy. I have come that they may have life and have it to the full. I am the Good Shepherd. The Good Shepherd lays down his life for the sheep. The hired hand is not the shepherd and does not own the sheep. So when he sees the wolf coming, he abandons the sheep and runs away. Then the wolf attacks the flock and scatters it. The man runs away because he is a hired hand and cares nothing for the sheep. I am the Good Shepherd. I know my sheep, and my sheep know me—just as the Father knows me, and I know the Father—and I lay down my life for the sheep. I have other sheep that are not of this sheep pen. I must bring them also. They too will listen to my voice, and there shall be one flock and one shepherd. The reason my Father loves me is that I lay down my life—only to take it up again. No one takes it from me, but I lay it

down of my own accord. I have authority
to lay it down and authority to take it up
again. This command I received from my
Father. (John 10:10–18 NIV)

I am glad to know that when my back is against the
wall, I have Jesus there to have my back and to fight my battle for me. I know that no matter what happens to me in this
life that as long as I keep God first, He won't make me last,
that I will stay winning the small battles because Jesus has
already won the war.

The enemy will have you to think that this is false,
but it is not false. Jesus laid down His life for all of us. And
because of that, we don't have to live in a defeated mentality.
We can have a victorious mentality because we know that
even though we have to go through in this life, as we lean on
and trust the Holy Trinity, there is no loss in us.

As God reigns victorious, so do we right along with
Him as long as we stay strong and firm and faint not. We
can't quit even though we get tired of the struggles and the
test and the trials in this life. We just can't afford to give up.
As we read the Word of God and we fast and pray and put
the whole armor of God on daily, let us remember that the
attacks of the enemy may appear great, but God is greater.

Don't allow the enemy to continue to take and take
from you in this life. Notice the enemy/foe, who and what
he is—a jealous foe of the Lord—and remember, it's just a
mirage. You have this with God. You win, I win, we win!

KINDNESS GOES A LONG WAY

As a child of the Most High God, there are things that are expected out of us, and it shows whose we are when we display it. Compassion is one, and so is kindness. We must be respectful to ourselves and those around us. We must not take delight in things of the world, like gossip and lying on others.

When people come to us with some juicy tea to spill about other people, we need to turn them away and simply say, "Hey, so and so, that is none of my business. But if you feel that so and so is going through a hard time right now, we can go into prayer for them right now if you would like too."

I promise you that if you start doing that, they will not be so quick to come to you with the foolery and mess that they are trying to keep up. God holds His children at a certain standard, and we need to make sure, as faithful followers of Jesus, our Lord, that we uphold it. As disciple of Jesus, we need not to ever steer away from our root, which is through Jesus Christ, our Lord.

We have to listen to the word of God and be doers of the word. I cannot reiterate this enough that just listening to and or reading the Word of God isn't enough. We have to allow that word to take root in our heart and be worked out in our lives. We must be humble and remain that way no matter how we are evolving and elevating in this life.

It is not the will of God that any of His children think or feel that they are better than the next, because it was the grace of God that has spared us all. If it had not been for God's mercy and grace, where would any of us be? So we have to remember where we came from and how we all got over and don't look down on those who are not there yet.

We need to have the same compassion in us to help them and pray for them that God had to see us through our dark era. We need to know our place and don't overstep our boundaries when dealing with others.

As people come to us with so-called information and their so-called seeking help for others, we need to consider the source of who it is that we are dealing with. Because people will try to bait you into talking to them or with them about another person and will use what you say against you or twist it to start drama with you and the next person.

Be careful to only speak when you feel God has a word for you to say. And when you don't know what to say, simply just don't say a word. It's okay to say, "You know I don't know about that. Let me pray on it, and I'll get back to you." In doing this, you can save yourself from giving unrighteous and unorthodox advice to others that can potentially confuse them and or turn them away from God.

We are to be examples to each other. We have to make sure we are mindful of what we say and do daily, and that in whatever we do or say to others, we are showing love and kindness. My granny used to say, "Look, hun, a little kindness can go a very long way. You never know what a person may be going through. What you say and do when you are interacting with them that day can make a great difference in their life."

The Word of God says a lot about how we need to be toward one another and how we need to speak to each other. Let's explore some of what it says.

> Death and life are in the power of the tongue: and they that love it shall eat the fruit thereof. (Proverbs 18:21KJV)

> One with knowledge restrains his words, and a discerning person stays calm. (Proverbs 17:27 TLV)

> The Lord detests evil plans, but he delights in pure words. (Proverbs 15:26 NLT)

> Everyone enjoys a fitting reply; it is wonderful to say the right thing at the right time! (Proverbs 15:23NLT)

These are just a few of many scriptures in the Bible that speak on using your words wisely when dealing with each other. I remember as a child hearing story of the boy who cried wolf. He was bored and decided to play a trick on the village people, so he used his words inappropriately to trick them into believing that he needed help so much, until one day, danger was really there, and his word meant nothing, and his sheep were slaughtered by the wolf.

We need to be kind to each other and use our words wisely and not to trick and or manipulate people into doing what it is that we want them to do. I have a motto that I have tried to use all my life, and that is, if I can't help you, I won't hurt you. This is how I have chosen to live my life.

I would like to say, well it has brought me nothing but peace and prosperity, but that would be a lie. I hold fast to this motto because I know it's expected of me, and I chose to live this way. But everyone doesn't feel the same way. We see that there are plenty of people in this world who choose to be evil and allow their words and actions to hurt others on a daily basis.

This is where the children of God come in as we see the people of this world for who and what they are, and we are trying to show love, kindness, and compassion to people in a world that live in the darkness. We are supposed to be the beacon of light that those who seek change need to see to receive that change.

How can they see that change if we are the same way that the people in the world are? We were called apart for a reason. We are different for a reason, and we all need to know that kindness is important for the work we have been called to do. I have heard so many people say, "Well I'm going to treat people the way they treat me. Whatever they give to me, I'm going to give it back to them." Well that's okay if you are not a child of the Most High God. That's fine if you don't care about other people's feelings. But if you are a child of God, you have to treat people the way You want to be treated, not the way they treat you. People also say, "Oh well, that's not fair," and I agree. But life isn't fair.

When you chose to become a child of God, or at least I hope you chose to come to God of your own free will, you accepted the fact that you would no longer be of this world but live in it until the return of Jesus. Since you chose this, and since I've chosen to be a child of God and a disciple of Jesus, we have to follow the way, the path, that Jesus paved for all of us.

There is no way around it. We have to show love. We have to show compassion. We have to show the same mercy we've received from God for our many mistakes to others. What is going to hurt to be kind? What is going to hurt to show love to someone? Will your life be turned inside out if you showed compassion for those who others have looked passed?

Where would any of us be if God never showed us compassion or had mercy on us? Are we that perfect now that we forgot that we once were in a loathly dark place before we came to Jesus? Can you take a look back over your life and see where God has brought you from and still not show kindness?

I know I can't, and it's part of the reason why I am writing this book. God has showed me so much mercy and grace and compassion that I want all of you to know it's okay to be down and out, but you don't have to stay there. For all of you who are reading this right now and you who are believers, you have to, I have to, we have to show more love, more kindness, more mercy, and more compassion to others daily.

For those who may be reading this, and you need to read this, know that God loves you, and you have to surround yourself around those who speak life to you. You have to start speaking life to yourself, and you have to change those you are around and the way you live. Come out of the darkness into the marvelous light. You will be glad that you did.

Chapter 14

WHO CALLED YOU?

I remember a time when I was living with my granny on Maple in Maywood before she moved back to Mississippi. I was lying there in the front room on the rollaway bed. I was sleeping when I heard her call my name. I said, "Ma'am?" there was no answer, so I drifted off back to sleep. I heard my name being called again, and I said, "Ma'am?" yet again, no answer, so I drifted off back to sleep. I heard my name being called a third time, so I jumped up and ran in her room. But when I got in there, she was fast asleep. I kind of shook it off and let it pass, that I was dream. And the next morning, I talked to her. I asked her.

I said, "Hey, Granny, did you call me last night?"

She said, "No, I didn't. It wasn't me."

So who was it that called me that woke me up out my sleep three times? I thought it was her. But she confirmed that it wasn't. So who then was it that had called my name that night? That stayed with me a very long time. I was doing a Bible study some years later, and I came across 1 Samuel 3, and the hair stood straight up on the back of my neck and arms. I read it and said, "Oh my god!" First Samuel 3 (NIV) says:

The Lord Calls Samuel

> The boy Samuel ministered before the Lord under Eli. In those days, the word of the Lord was rare; there were not many visions. One night, Eli, whose eyes were becoming so weak that he could barely see, was lying down in his usual place.
>
> The lamp of God had not yet gone out, and Samuel was lying down in the house of the Lord where the ark of God was. Then the Lord called Samuel. Samuel answered, "Here I am." And he ran to Eli and said, "Here I am. You called me." But Eli said, "I did not call. Go back and lie down." So he went and lay down. Again the Lord called, "Samuel!" And Samuel got up and went to Eli and said, "Here I am. You called me." "My son," Eli said, "I did not call. Go back and lie down." Now Samuel did not yet know the Lord: The word of the Lord had not yet been revealed to him. A third time, the Lord called, "Samuel!" And Samuel got up and went to Eli and said, "Here I am. You called me." Then Eli realized that the Lord was calling the boy. So Eli told Samuel, "Go and lie down, and if he calls you, say, 'Speak, Lord, for your servant is listening.'" So Samuel went and

lay down in his place. The Lord came and stood there, calling as at the other times, "Samuel! Samuel!"

Then Samuel said, "Speak, for your servant is listening."

And the Lord said to Samuel: "See, I am about to do something in Israel that will make the ears of everyone who hears about it tingle. At that time, I will carry out against Eli everything I spoke against his family—from beginning to end. For I told him that I would judge his family forever because of the sin he knew about. His sons blasphemed God, and he failed to restrain them. Therefore I swore to the house of Eli, the guilt of Eli's house will never be atoned for by sacrifice or offering.'"

Samuel lay down until morning and then opened the doors of the house of the Lord. He was afraid to tell Eli the vision, but Eli called him and said, "Samuel, my son."

Samuel answered, "Here I am."

"What was it he said to you?" Eli asked. "Do not hide it from me. May God deal with you, be it ever so severely if you hide from me anything he told you." So Samuel told him everything, hiding nothing from him. Then Eli said, "He is the Lord, let him do what is good in his eyes." The Lord was with Samuel as he grew up, and he let none of Samuel's

words fall to the ground. And all Israel
from Dan to Beersheba recognized that
Samuel was attested as a prophet of the
Lord. The Lord continued to appear at
Shiloh, and there he revealed himself to
Samuel through his word.

I read this and felt troubled in my spirit, and I said I
wish I had known this sooner. What if it was God that was
calling me, and I might have missed my opportunity to help
myself or to help somebody else? I would like to say that that
was the only time that I missed hearing from God. He had
to teach me how to hear His voice and know that it is Him
that is calling me.

You might be wondering, *Well how in the world can that
happen?* He does it as you study and meditate on His Word.
As you seek His face, the more He will reveal Himself to
you. And the deeper the relationship you have with Him, the
better it will be for you to determine who it is that is calling
you and/or trying to get your attention. I would like to say
to you that not everything you may hear may be the ushering
of the Holy Spirit, so you have to be very careful. The Bible
says that the enemy can trick you, so we have to test the spirit
by its fruit. Is what being asked of you in the Word of God
it something that you know God would say to you or ask of
you? The Bible says in Matthew 7:15–20 (NIV):

True and False Prophets

Watch out for false prophets. They come
to you in sheep's clothing, but inwardly
they are ferocious wolves. By their fruit,
you will recognize them. Do people pick

grapes from thornbushes or figs from thistles? Likewise, every good tree bears good fruit, but a bad tree bears bad fruit. A good tree cannot bear bad fruit, and a bad tree cannot bear good fruit. Every tree that does not bear good fruit is cut down and thrown into the fire. Thus by their fruit, you will recognize them.

God always tells us to make sure we know who it is that we allow to speak a word over us or to us. We are so quick to receive a word that we let ourselves vulnerable and open to attacks from the enemy. I have a friend. I can say she is more than a friend; she is more like a sister. One day I was having some issues with my husband, shook my life, period. And I sought her out for prayer and advice.

I started telling her what was going on, then I told her about some advice someone had told me.

She said, "Well can I ask you a question?

And I said, "Sure."

She said, "The person that came to you and gave you that advice, would you trade lives with them?"

I sat back and looked and said, "Well no."

And she said, "Well in that case, why would you take advice from them? I encourage you to consider the source of the people that you talk to."

When she told me that, I was like, "Wow, okay. I never thought about it like that." And ever since then, I have been applying that to my life. Whenever God tries to tell us something, whether He does it directly or through other people, we need to pay attention and make sure we are listening.

So many times, God would be speaking to us, and we would ignore what He was saying for whatever reason it may be at the time. But there ought to not ever be a time when we are not willing to listen to God and what He has to say. Just the other day, I was talking to my oldest daughter, and I was telling her that she was a walking, talking miracle.

A few months back, my daughter and a couple of her friends were in a really bad car wreck. The vehicle they were in flipped and went air-bound. None of them had seat belts on. She hit the windshield and flew head first out of the passenger window, and it was up. When her friend called and told me that my daughter was in a bad wreck and she wasn't breathing, I almost lost my mind.

I heard in my spirit, "Calm down and pray," so I did, and thanks to the fact my daughter put an app on all of our phones so we could find each other. We were able to find her. I got to the scene and saw the car. I was like, there can't be any survivors because the truck was totaled and upside down. I just said, "Jesus, please let my baby be okay. The EMT told me to go to the hospital. They were stabilizing her, and they would be there shortly.

I was praying all the way there that she would be whole, that nothing would be found. My oldest son had made it there before her dad, and I made it. We were led to a waiting room for the family, and we all began to pray some more. They had a chaplain to come to talk to us, and she prayed with us, and she was the go in between for a while.

The doctor came in and said, "We ran every test. she has no broken bones."

We just knew her skull was going to be cracked, but nothing, no internal bleeding—nothing—just a really severe concussion. And her right knee was swollen and bruised. She had several gashes and cuts in her face and head on the right side, but the trauma surgeon did an excellent job sewing her up. The other girls were fine—just a few scratches.

The other two girls got to go home that day, but my daughter had to stay in the hospital for a week. My daughter went through an ordeal. She really had a hard time. And that accident, I can say, changed her perspective on life. She had a carnal knowledge about God and the Holy Trinity, but it wasn't until she had this accident that she got to see for herself that God is real and that angels exist because they were there with her that day, and they saved her life. The trauma surgeon came in the room and said, "Mother, I can honestly say that with the condition of the car and how your daughter flew out the window, I was expecting for her to have internal injuries, broken bones, and an open skull with her brain out. I cannot explain to you how she made it and with little to no injury. Besides this concussion, all I can say is that she is a very, very lucky girl,"

I said, "No, it was a miracle. She's a miracle. She has been through a whole lot in her life and survived it all, and she has survived this. God is keeping her. He has an awesome plan for her life."

Before the accident, I just kept saying, "Li'l girl, get your life in order. Fix your relationship with God. And if you don't have one, get one."

But of course, she did what she felt she wanted to. I pray for my children and trust God to keep and protect my children. I listen when He tells me what to do and when to do it.

I try to teach my kids to do the same thing. But sometimes they aren't going to listen, and that's okay because we are all on our own individual journey in this life, and she had to find out for herself that she needs to start listening to God and truly know when God is speaking to her.

Chapter 15

Don't Allow You to Stop You

I was about to do this very thing. I had started to write this book and somehow allowed the enemy to sneak in to discourage me not to finish. Yes, this book was about to start collecting dust as well. I have a bad habit of talking myself out of things, but I couldn't do it because the Holy Spirit let me know that this book isn't about me.

This book is for the people so that you all will know that God is and because He is you are , and we can face all things that we go through and make it through. The enemy doesn't take time off from attacking us, and we should never take a vacation spiritually. I cannot afford to give up on me or for you all.

I have to keep pressing my way through, and I implore you all to keep pressing your way through no matter how hard it gets because we got this. I got this. You got this. Now that I got that out the way, let's talk about why its import that you don't allow yourself to stop you. I learned in this life that no one in this world will go harder for you and your life than you will.

I have a huge family, and you would think that we would be solid. But when push came to shove, it was family that let me down the most in my life. I can't even count how many times I've had to go to the Lord in prayer to help me, because everyone, even my mother, had proven to be untrustworthy at the time.

I felt so alone in this world. And how many know that it is at this point in our lives that the enemy hits us the hardest because we are at our most vulnerable. God has showed me, time and time again in my life, that with all the unsteady people in my life, He has and will never change up on me.

I can never recall a time when I called on Him that He didn't show up, whether it was right then and there or in His own perfect timing, He always showed up and came to my rescue. I know that if He has done this for me and I'm not perfect, He will do the same for you.

Isn't it wonderful that you can come to God just as you are, and He accepts and loves you through the growing and teaching stage? He will never abandon you or talk about you or make you feel unworthy of His love and acceptance. That is not the God we serve. He loves us and loves on us while He is correct and teaching His ways.

If then we know that He is not condemning us but welcoming us into His loving arms, what is stopping us but us. Let it go. You can't change one single thing in your past, and it is over. But you can better your life for your future. You can start making the steps to being the best you that you can be. You can change where you go and who you surround yourself around. You have the power to control who you allow in your inner circle.

We ought to let go and let God have His way with our lives and in our lives. Ask yourself, "How am I stopping myself from growing mentally, emotionally, and spiritually? Whatever the reason for you stopping yourself, it's not worth it. I know life is hard. I have seen my share of hardships. But guess what, by the grace of God, I'm still here. You are still here, and that's a plus. That means that we still have a chance to get this thing right.

It doesn't rain all the time. The sun does shine. And if you give Him a chance, the Son will shine in your life through your life. The same peace that God gives me, I pray you receive that peace and pick yourself up and realize that you matter in this life. You are important to God, and you are important to me. And that's why I am writing this book because I care about my brothers and sisters in Christ.

I love you all because He showed compassion for me and loved me when I never thought that anyone would. I am here writing these words because God loved me and spared me and had mercy on me and had helped me change my life and my outlook on life and the people in it.

I know it gets hard to remember this when you are going through something, but we all have to remember that in the Bible, it says in Ephesians 6:12 (AMP):

> For our struggle is not against flesh and blood (contending only with physical opponents) but against the rulers, against the powers, against the world forces of this (present) darkness, against the spiritual forces of wickedness in the heavenly (supernatural) places.

Yes, people will get on your very last nerve, but it's the negative influences that is working through them. And if we don't stay connected to God and the Holy Trinity, we can be negatively influenced to do the same to other people. I heard a gospel song by Yolanda Adams, and she said this battle is not yours, it's the Lord's.

Since we know that we need to allow Him to fix it, then we need to just be obedient to His will, His Word, and to His way and not allow anything, not even ourselves, to prevent us from living a life that is pleasing to God and beneficial to each other. I also have been told that self-care is a must in this life, that if I neglect to take care of myself, I can't help anyone. So self-preservation isn't being selfish, it is a necessity.

If we are not our best, we can't be what we need to be for the people God placed along out path in the journey called life. We can't neglect our physical health or our mental and emotional health, and we especially can't neglect our spiritual health. God wants us to be sharp and aware like a fine-tuned instrument, ready to be played by the Master.

Just as how we are good to others and do for them, we need to set aside some of that care and compassion for ourselves. We need to forgive ourselves and love ourselves and encourage ourselves and know that we too are deserving of the love that we issue out to others.

I've been telling myself for years that I need to take better care of myself. I need to make sure I am okay because I will just empty myself out to people and feel drained and emotionally bankrupt. I learned that the more time I spend with God, the more He replenishes me and fills my empty cup. He is there, ready and willing to be all that we need when we need Him.

I assure there is no safer place than in the arms of God. He is not far at all, and He is always listening. You never have to worry about calling Him and Him not being there for you. He is always available for you and for me. We just can't allow us to stop ourselves from reaching out and up to the only help we know.

Chapter 16

GOD CHOSE YOU

I remember growing up, I felt different from my siblings. To me, I was normal. But I was told a lot, "Girl, you are strange," or "Girl, you care too much," or this one, which is my favorite one, "Why are you always trying to help everybody?"

I personally felt that the people around me were odd, and I was the normal one. Because how could you wake up and not be happy that you are alive? How could you wake up and look outside and not see God in nature and hear Him in the crickets, chirping.

I was in love with Jesus, and I was in love with nature and the animals in it. I would see a wounded animal and pray for it. I was always happy. And even though I didn't feel love in my home, and I was bullied at school, I somehow knew that I was loved by God. And that was all that mattered.

The Word of God says that we are to guard our hearts.

> Keep and guard your heart with all vigilance and above all that you guard, for out

of it flows the springs of life. (Proverbs
4:23 AMPC)

As a child, I didn't know how to do this. I thought it
was up to my mother to teach me and/or to pray for a shield
of protection to be around me as a youth until I was better
able to understand how to seek God and do it for myself.

At the age of forty-one, I can honestly tell you why God
said that we were to do this. Because people can drain you,
and life can drain you. The enemy can send so many things
your way if you don't know how to protect yourself, and it
will destroy your faith.

I remember so vividly that girl that was so in love with
God and life, and I looked back over my life and saw how
having such a good heart and no guidance allowed life to
chew me up and spit me out. It made me shut down and
draw myself from the world. But this is not what God wants
for His people.

Thus it's why He said that we are to guard, to protect,
our hearts, because out of it springs forth life. If we do not
care, we will fall for every trap set by the enemy to ensure that
we fail. A little while back here, I was so hurt from dedicating
myself to helping people and trying to be their go-to person
that I got burned out.

I was used and mistreated because my heart was big,
and my desire to help superseded my ability to see that people's intentions were not the best toward me. I gave myself
and gave until I was empty, and I kept asking God, "What's
wrong with me? God, why do I feel so drained?"

I didn't know that as we pour out to people, we are
supposed to go to God—not man, but to God—to get filled
and not just to get filled a little. We are to get filled until it

overflows. And we are to help others with the overflow to ensure that we never run empty.

The emptiness comes from when we look to ourselves and other people to do for us what only God can do. So then how can one get replenished when they give and give? Well the answer to that is simple: Stay prayerful. Read your Word daily, attend services, or listen to the Word as often as you can.

Seek God continuously and fast and pray. If your peace isn't important to you, guess what, it will not be important to anyone else either. You have to make sure you are covered and cared for before you can help others.

All of this, I said, "Well why me, God?" And for the hundredth time, He was like, "Why not you? Who are you that you can't be tested, tried, and go through? If Jesus, who is my only begotten son, went through and was tested and tried, why can't you be?"

When I heard these words, I became saddened, and I said, "I am sorry. I just got tired."

"I heard those whom I have called. I predestined and know you, so I know what you can and cannot do, what you are and aren't capable of, and I will strengthen you and give you the power to withstand all and do what I called you to do."

Okay, once again I was stuck, looking crazy like, "Lord, okay, so when is all of this supposed to happen? You said You called to do a work for You. So when does this supposed to transpire?"

I just heard, "In due season."

All I know is that God is going to do it. I don't know when. All I know is that I am to trust Him and obey. If you know for a fact that God has called you, then don't allow anyone, including yourself, to stop you from walking in that calling. I know tidbits of information of what it is that I am to be doing, and I trust that God will show me more and more as I open myself up to Him and His will and His way. We serve a Mighty God and trust that whatever it is that we need, He will supply.

Chapter 17

WITH AN OPEN HEART

The Word of God says in Matthew 22:34–40 (NIV):

The Greatest Commandment

> Hearing that Jesus had silenced the Sadducees, the Pharisees got together. One of them, an expert in the law, tested Him with this question: "Teacher, which is the greatest commandment in the Law?" Jesus replied: "'Love the Lord your God with all your heart and with all your soul and with all your mind.' This is the first and greatest commandment. And the second is like it: 'Love your neighbor as yourself.' All the law and the prophets hang on these two commandments."

I was told all my life that God was love, so I believed that when I took the time to care about people and love them that I was doing the will of God. It wasn't until I got older that I realized that in loving God, I had to establish a relationship with Him and not just people. In 2001, I did just that. I took out the time. I think it was about six months to study the Word of God and learn who He was and who I was in Him.

I learned that I had to be freed to be on this journey of faith and wisdom. What I mean by that is I had to be delivered from all the bad things that I had been through in my life that had allowed my heart to be hardened. It was hard for me to get past some things, like the hurt I experienced from my mom not being there for me the way that I needed her to be.

That, I feel, was the biggest issue at the time. I just couldn't understand, especially with being a mother, how a mother could bring forth life in this world and not love them and care for them properly. I had two children, and I was truly struggling to live and provide for them. But I fought tooth and nail to do it. I asked God many times, growing up, what was so bad about me that I didn't deserve to be loved.

As I sought Him out, the Lord told me what I needed to know about my situations in my past as he healed me from them. And it's important that I tell you that I allowed Him to heal me. There are a lot of people out here that think that when they pray, God just fixes it. But it doesn't quite work like that.

I learned that you have to yield your will to the ushering of the Holy Spirit in order for it to work on you, in you, and through you. You have to do your part and submit yourself to the Lord as a living sacrifice. You have to go in the relationship with an open heart and an open mind to change.

God is not going to force Himself on you or force healing in your life. You have to get up and grab it through genuine confession, repentance, and faith. I was tired of being sad and unhappy, and I was ready to be set free from all the things in my life that had me bound.

The Word of God says in Matthew 9:29 (NKJV):

> Then He touched their eyes, saying, "According to your faith, let it be to you."

We are blessed, and we receive the things we seek God for through our faith. I remember my granny used to say, "Child, if you just have faith of a mustard seed, you can move a mountain." I had so many mountains in my life that I need great faith to move, but I just didn't know how to work my faith yet.

I knew that everything that I needed was in that book that I was studying and reading—the Word of God—and applying it to my life has brought me a mighty long way. And I know that as I keep reading and keep applying the word of God to my life, it will continue to excel me, elevating me higher and higher in the Lord.

Because of the fact that I have been through a lot in my young life, I have been able to talk to people about a lot of situations. One situation where I had to have an open heart to be able to heal was when I was going through domestic violence.

My daughter's father would beat me just because another man looked and smile and/or showed any type of interest in me because he was insecure. I would pray, "God, please help me get out of this situation." And for years it happened, and I became upset with God and felt that He wanted me to suffer, or He just didn't care when that wasn't the case at all.

As I was being inflicted, I was reminded of this verse: "When an impure spirit comes out of a person, it goes through arid places, seeking rest and does not find it. Then it says, 'I will return to the house I left.' When it arrives, it finds the house unoccupied, swept clean, and put in order. Then it goes and takes with it seven other spirits more wicked than itself, and they go in and live there. And the final condition of that person is worse than the first. That is how it will be with this wicked generation."

I just fell to my knees and had to repent. I was then showed all the times God got me away and all the times I went back or allowed him to come back because I thought he would change, and every time it got worse and worse until he almost took my life.

The God I serve had other plans for my life and wouldn't allow the enemy to kill me. I had to open my heart to God and ask that he take the pain away and take the soul ties that this man brought into my life away so that I could be free to move forward and never look back.

It's been almost twelve years, and I have never looked back nor have I had a desire to do so. I am not going to lie and say that it's been easy because it hasn't been. It's been a long journey. And since then, God has blessed me with a spouse. And the enemy has been trying to work his way up and in my marriage. But I see him, and I fight. We must never ever give up or in.

We must never allow the enemy to have more power over us as children of God than the Spirit of the Lord has over us. Let us then remember that with an open heart, with a repentant heart, with an accepting heart, we should come to the Father. When we can't trust in anyone else, we can rest assured that we can fully trust in the Lord, and He will always be there to love and take care of all His children.

Chapter 18

FIGHT

I know that I am not the only one that has heard this scripture from 2 Chronicles 20:14–16 (NIV):

> Then the Spirit of the Lord came on Jahaziel, son of Zechariah, the son of Benaiah, the son of Jeiel, the son of Mattaniah, a Levite and descendant of Asaph, as he stood in the assembly. He said: "Listen, King Jehoshaphat, and all who live in Judah and Jerusalem! This is what the Lord says to you: 'Do not be afraid or discouraged because of this vast army. For the battle is not yours but God's. Tomorrow, march down against them. They will be climbing up by the Pass of Ziz, and you will find them at the end of the gorge in the Desert of Jeruel."

God is always ready and willing to fight our battles for us. We are never alone along our Christian journey, even when it feels like it, or the enemy tries to feed you this lie. When you made the choice to come to God just as you were and to become a child of His to be born again, you came into a multitude of heaven's army of angels that are ready to go to war for you at the request of God.

They are ready to fight with you, and God will give you power through the Holy Spirit to accomplished any and everything that you need in this life.

> I have fought the good fight, I have fin-
> ished the race, I have kept the faith. (2
> Timothy 4:7 NIV)

We just have to hang on in there and faint not. I know how hard times can be. There were many times in my life that I just think that I could make it. I was ready to throw in the towel, and I would always hear in my spirit, "Fight."

The Bible says in 1 Corinthians 9:24 (TLV):

> Don't you know that in a stadium, the
> runners all run, but one receives the
> prize? Run in such a way that you may
> win!

God is rooting for us to make it. He wants us all to win but knows the road is a tough one. He knows the obstacles that we will face, but He is always there to see us through them all. Typing these words, I could hear my granny say, "Ain't no quitting in me." I never understood what she meant by that until I got older and start being hit by the pressures of life.

I had a family that was depending on me. I had to fight for them, if not for myself. I couldn't afford to have any quit in me either. In Isaiah 40:29–31 (NIV), it says:

> He gives strength to the weary and increases the power of the weak. Even youths grow tired and weary, and young men stumble and fall; but those who hope in the Lord will renew their strength. They will soar on wings like eagles; they will run and not grow weary; they will walk and not be faint.

We don't ever have to worry about wasting time fighting the good fight like most people have said. I used to hear when I was a babe in Christ, "Girl, you're too young to be trying to live like that. You're wasting all your time at home reading your Bible, and life is passing you by. Get out, have fun, and live."

I am not going to lie. I sat at home after hearing that. I tried to live like other people, but it just didn't feel right. So I would always come back to the things of God. The people of the world will have their reward, and the Bible says this about the saints of God in Galatians 6:9 (NIV):

> Let us not become weary in doing good, for at the proper time, we will reap a harvest if we do not give up.

Whatever seeds we sow in this life—good or bad—we will reap the harvest. Then if you know that you are doing what you know is right, you don't have anything you worry about, because God will always have His hands on you and see you through all that you face in this life.

James 1:12 (NIV) tells us this:

> Blessed is the one who perseveres under trial because, having stood the test, that person will receive the crown of life that the Lord has promised to those who love him.

God will never walk away from us or turn a deaf ear to our prayers. This I guarantee that we can be confident in. If you have trusted others, and they have let you down, know that what you do for the kingdom of God is not a waste and that He is always trustworthy.

> I can do all this through Him who gives me strength. (Philippians 4:13 NIV)

When we get excited about God, God is excited with us and is pleased when we glorify His holy name. We serve a faithful, loving, and caring God who loves us and wants to see us prosper and not fail. He is our number one cheerleader when it comes to our lives.

He knows who we are and who He created us to be. So He is most definitely rooting for us to walk in our purpose for Him and continue to fight the good fight in the mighty name of Jesus because we know that the battle is already won.

We tend to get mad with God when we try to do things our own way, and it doesn't pan out the way that we want it to, and we find ourselves yet again on the battlefield and screaming, "Woe is me!" Most times, we open doors in our lives that should have remained closed.

God will do one of two things when we do this: He can either see us through it or deliver us from it. But no matter what, He makes sure we learn from it so that we don't keep going through the same things again.

> 11 No discipline seems pleasant at the time but painful. Later on, however, it produces a harvest of righteousness and peace for those who have been trained by it. (Hebrews 12:11 NIV)

Let's fight our battles, knowing that we can come out on top if we allow the spirit of God to work on us, in us, and through us. Your journey in this life can be as hard and/or tough as you allow it to be. I know this much because I have had a hard, hard road, and I can admit that it was mostly because I wanted to do it the Candice way.

As children of the Most High God, we need to understand that what we do for God and His kingdom is what is important and is what matters and count the most. We can never live to please man because man is never satisfied. We run around this world like a chicken with our heads cut off to make people happy. But God said in Colossians 3:23–24 (TLV):

> Whatever you do, work at it from the soul as for the Lord and not for people. For you know that from the Lord, you will receive the inheritance as a reward. It is to the Lord Messiah you are giving service.

We need to live this life to please God more and people less. And when we do this, the people that are in real need of what God has to offer will receive what it is that they need from the children of God. And while they are fighting their battles, they too will see God in the midst of their struggle.

What you do today matters. You matter. And what we do for God and His kingdom matters. In the book of Matthew 11:28 (TLV), it says:

> Come to Me, all who are weary and bur-
> dened, and I will give you rest.

Matthew 19:26 (NIV) says:

> Jesus looked at them and said, "With
> man, this is impossible. But with God,
> all things are possible."

Not only are we assured that as we fight along this jour-ney that God will be there to see us through and guarantee us the victory, but we know that it is through His might and His power and not our own that we will accomplish all things.

We are not alone. You are not alone. I know I am not alone. We can succeed in all that we go through if we just trust and believe. Where is the fight in you? You cannot just give up or in. The Word says in Jeremiah 29:11 (NIV):

> For I know the plans I have for you,"
> declares the Lord, "plans to prosper you
> and not to harm you, plans to give you
> hope and a future.

Every scripture that I have given you here states how you and I were born to win. God knew that Satan was going to try to make our lives a living hell. So God, in all His mercy and grace, supplied us with all that we need through reading the Word of God and applying it to our lives to let us know that we are not our situations and circumstances. We are way better than them. We are champions. We are victors. And we stand victorious in all that we do if we just don't give up and continue to fight. You don't have to take my word for it. The Bible is full of people that overcame because they trusted God.

David spoke in the book of Psalm about all the things that he faced and how he was leaning on God to see him through it all. He knew he messed up a lot, like we all do. But where he differs from some of us, he never gave up on doing what he needed to do for God.

> Though he may stumble, he will not fall,
> for the Lord upholds him with his hand.
> (Psalm 37:24 NIV)

As long as we continue fighting the good fight, God will keep upholding us with His hand.

Chapter 19

WHY NOT YOU

How many times have you gone through something in this life, and you whispered under your breath or even out loud, "Lord, our God, why me?" I know I have said this numerous times in my life. I have also said, "Lord, if it's not one thing, it's another," or "Lord, how long?"

As I sit here and write these words, the situations flood back to me for the reasons why I had to say those very words. I feel so grateful that the Lord, our God, saw fit to see me through all of that, and He is still here with me, standing here, seeing me through so much more.

I don't know about you, but I tend to start out with the best intentions to do what it is that God wants and needs for me to do. But somehow, someway, I end up failing God or coming up short. Instead of Him giving up on me, telling me, "I'm tired of you, Candice," He always tells me, "Candice, get up and get back in the race."

He has told me this way too much for me to even count. It wasn't because I didn't want to do it, it was because God saw the best in me even when I didn't see the best in myself.

I would count myself out because I felt that I could never live up to this person that God created me to be, because this person was not perfect, and I wanted to be perfect for God. It was and is my desire to be to God all He had and has been to me. I didn't want to keep failing Him.

I am brought back to when he revealed to me who I was in him, and I said, "Why me?" And He spoke to my spirit and said, "Why not you? If I called you to it, I know you can do it if you set yourself aside and allow my Spirit to abide in you."

I was like, "Oh, okay." But notice that He was telling me, "I know that you cannot accomplish these things through your own might."

I want you to utilize the power of the Holy Spirit that dwells in you to accomplish these things. For it is only through my power that all things are possible that seem impossible for man. Then I would have an "Oh, I see now" God moment. God wants us to start relying more on Him to accomplish things in our lives.

I know that I have shared with you all how I was abused and how my daughter got taken from me by my abusive family. And I later found out that she too was being abused. That situation, I found it hard to forgive the man that abused me and the people who had hurt my daughter as well.

I am not going to lie to you, I hated those people, and I wished they perished. I didn't really care about the abuse I sustained, but I was more concerned with how a person could hurt a child like that. How evil do you have to be to inflict pain on an innocent child like that? God brought to my spirit that it is hurting people that hurt other people. And even though it is not right that they do it, it is the reason why so many hurt others.

I didn't want to hear that at the time. I was tired of going through the foolishness in my life. It was one horrible event right after the next. I was like, "My God, can I get a break here? Why me, Lord? What have I done in my young life to upset you so? When will life get better for me?"

Once again God spoke into my spirit, "Candice, why not you? Are you then better than my only begotten Son, Jesus?"

I said, "No I am not. I cannot even come close." Did He not suffer and have to endure hardships and hatred from people that was not merited? Didn't it even cost Him His life?

I was like, "Yes."

He said, "So then, why not you? You too must suffer as My Son suffered. And like My Son, you too will overcome it all, just as long as you do what you know is right and not give up."

You have to understand how hard this was to go through everything that I went through and was going through having to hear the Lord say, "Okay, enough soaking. Get up and press forward. This too shall pass." I wasn't always willing to get up and move forward as He would instruct me to.

There were times when I just stayed there in my misery and my sorrow, feeling sorry for myself and missing out on many blessings and wasted so much time. But ain't it good that God never gives up on us and don't allow us to give up on ourselves or our calling?

He was right there, speaking to me, "Get up, daughter. Get up, Candice," until I say, "I'm so sorry, Lord. Here I am. Help me please." And like the loving, caring Father that He is, *He* was right there to help me.

God is just that, a loving Father that is there for us even when we feel like we don't need God in our lives He is still there, caring for and loving us. Why not you? Why not me?

We are qualified through the Holy Spirit to do all things. And it is that same power that sees us through some of our toughest days.

Job was a faithful man to God. And no matter what afflictions that God allowed Him to suffer, He went through, knowing, trusting, that if the God that He served brought him to any of that, God would bring him out on top, even better than before. And God did just that.

God did that for Job, and God has done it for me. And He can do the same for you if you just trust and believe. Nobody said that this journey would be easy. I know that the Lord, our God, didn't bring me this far in life to leave me. The Word of God says in 1 John 4:4 (TLV):

> You are from God, children, and you have overcome them, because greater is He who is in you than he who is in the world.

We are His, and He is ours. And the love that He has for us is unimaginable. We will never be able to fully understand the capacity of the love that He has for us, but I am so glad that He loves me this much. I know that it was His love that has seen me through and that will continue to see me through.

I trust in Him for all things. And I pray everyone that picks up this book and reads these words learn to lean on the Lord, our God, and trust in Him like never before. He is waiting with open arms to love you and show you that He is all that you will or that I will ever need.

Chapter 20

Eyes Wide Shut

I was a very clumsy child growing up. I was always bumping into things that was apparently right there in front of me. But at the time, I couldn't see it. I ended up talking to the eye doctor, and they told me I needed glasses.

It wasn't that I was blind. It was just that I couldn't see that clearly, and I needed some help. And that's where the glasses came in. They allowed me to see clearly the things before me that I wouldn't have been able to see without them.

After receiving my glasses, I saw things that prevented me from tripping or falling and hurting myself. I saw the obstacles that were in my way and either moved them or went around them. The way I was in the natural, as I began my journey with the Lord, I discovered I was the same way in the spirit.

I was following Jesus with an uncertainty of the things in front of me. But as I open up myself to the ushering of the Holy Spirit, I began to see clearer the attacks of the enemy laid before me in my path.

Nowadays people are saying, "Get woke or be woke." But back then, it was "I just got a revelation." I found out that as you seek God's face in all matters, He will give you a revelation of the things that it is you who need to see, pertaining to His will and His purpose for your life and the lives of those whom He has set along your path for you to help.

This is how He operates. He doesn't just help us, lead us, and give us what we need. He equipped us to be able to help others along our journey. We are supposed to support and be there for each other. I pray for you, and you pray for me. I see you in need, and I help you. You see a need, and you help the person in need and so forth and so on.

We are His children, and that makes us all family. And what does family do, or what does a true family supposed to do? We are supposed to help each other, support each other, build one another up, and encourage each other.

Am I my brother's, my sister's keeper? Yes, I am. This is not the case. We, as the children of God, are not standing up and doing what it is that is expected from us, and that is mainly because we walk through this life with eyes wide shut.

We can't see the things that we need to see the way we need to see them. This is the case. Because we either need spiritual glasses, which is called the spirit of discernment, or we simply choose to not see. What is the spirit of discernment? You may ask.

Well I am glad that you asked. It is the ability to see and hear things in the spiritual realm in the natural through the power of the Holy Spirit. I had this gift as a young adult, and it sort of terrified me because I didn't understand at that time that when I saw or heard something, as a child, I was supposed to pray in the spirit about what I was seeing and sensing.

I began to ignore it because I didn't know how valuable the gift was. Shoot, I didn't know what a blessing it was to have all the gifts that I had. As an adult, I see clearer and seek the gift of the discernment daily so that I don't keep falling for the same traps. Walking in this life with our eyes shut leaves us vulnerable to the enemy.

I tell my kids how important it is to feed the natural body so that you don't go hungry. But it is equally as important that we feed our spirit as well. We have to be strong physically, mentally, emotionally, and spiritually.

We have to always be ready for anything that may come our way on a daily basis. When I wake up in the morning, I try to be conscious to always give God thanks, and I pray, "Thank You, Father God, for waking me up this morning and getting me started on my way. Thank You for waking all those that I know and love. And thank You for waking up those that I don't know this morning and getting them started on their way. For this is the day that the Lord has made. Let us rejoice and be glad, in Jesus's name. Amen.

I taught my kid this prayer. And then my son asked me, "Mom, why are you adding other people in your prayer?"

I told him, "It's to cover those that forgot to thank God this morning and for those who need God to watch over them, and they don't know Him yet."

He was like, "Oh, okay."

I was trying to get them in the habit of thinking of and lifting others before the Lord.

There was a saying that I heard a while back that said. "I don't know who's been praying for me, but I am sure glad that they did." People are in need of help all the time. Some don't know how to pray, so we can pray a prayer that will cover a multitude of people. Psalm 119:125 (TLV) says:

> I am Your servant. Give me discernment
> so I may understand Your testimonies.

Hosea 14:9 (AMP) says:

> 9: Whoever is (spiritually) wise, let him understand these things. Whoever is (spiritually) discerning and understanding, let him know them. For the ways of the Lord are right, and the righteous will walk in them. But transgressors will stumble and fall in them.

First Corinthians 2:14 (AMP) says:

> But the natural (unbelieving) man does not accept the things (the teachings and revelations) of the spirit of God, for they are foolishness (absurd and illogical) to him; and he is incapable of understanding them because they are spiritually discerned and appreciated (and he is unqualified to judge spiritual matters).

First Corinthians 12:10 (AMP) says:

> And to another the working of miracles, and to another prophecy (foretelling the future, speaking a new message from God to the people), and to another discernment of spirits (the ability to distinguish sound, godly doctrine from the deceptive doctrine of man-made religions and cults), to another various kinds of (unknown) tongues, and to another interpretation of tongues.

These are just a few scriptures that further lets us know that not only does the God that we serve want us to go through this life. With proper physical sight, He desires us to be able to see and/or sense things in the spirit as well. We don't have to walk in this life with eyes wide shut. For once, I was blind (spiritually), but now I see.

Chapter 21

WE WIN

When I was a child, there used to be a song that we sang in choir that used to say, "Victory and victory shall be mine. If I just hold peace and let the Lord fight my battles, victory shall be mine." Well of course, as a child, I had no idea what those word truly meant. I didn't know that I would have to hold on to those very words a lot in my life. There were several times in my life, as a young adult and an adult, where I have felt defeated. I felt that I may have messed up so bad in this life that there was no relief for me, that God had turned His back on me because He was tired of me messing up. But that was furthest from the truth. God didn't walk away from me, I detoured from His will, His purpose, and His plan for my life. I had come to the realization that throughout time, God has never lost one single battle. He has always come out on top. He has always been victorious. And all of those that trusted Him and obeyed Him and allowed Him to guide them were also victorious.

About the Author

Candice Rasco is a mother of four who has had a complicated and very spiritual life. She went through a lot of the hard knocks of life and experienced God's presence and miraculous power through it all. So she decided to share her experiences with the world in hopes that what she experienced and what she made through could help someone else become healed and an overcomer as well.

CPSIA information can be obtained
at www.ICGtesting.com
Printed in the USA
BVHW052152270522
638372BV00014B/117